Whale

Animal
Series editor: Jonathan Burt

Already published

Crow
Boria Sax

Bear
Robert E. Bieder

Tortoise
Peter Young

Parrot
Paul Carter

Cockroach
Marion Copeland

Rat
Jonathan Burt

Ant
Charlotte Sleigh

Snake
Drake Stutesman

Dog
Susan McHugh

Falcon
Helen Macdonald

Oyster
Rebecca Stott

Bee
Clare Preston

Forthcoming

Hare
Simon Carnell

Crocodile
Richard Freeman

Moose
Kevin Jackson

Spider
Katja and Sergiusz Michalskj

Fly
Steven Connor

Duck
Victoria de Rijke

Tiger
Susie Green

Salmon
Peter Coates

Fox
Martin Wallen

Wolf
Garry Marvin

Whale

Joe Roman

REAKTION BOOKS

For Debora Greger

Published by
REAKTION BOOKS LTD
33 Great Sutton Street
London EC1V ODX, UK
www.reaktionbooks.co.uk

First published 2006
Copyright © Joe Roman 2006

Printed and bound in Hong Kong

British Library Cataloguing in Publication Data

Roman, Joe
    Whale. – (Animal)
    1. Whales 2. Animals and civilization
    I. Title
    599.5

    ISBN 1 86189 246 2

Contents

1 First Surfacing

A column of mist splits the horizon, followed by a deep, unearthly sound, as if the ocean itself had come up for air. A bright glimmer flashes beneath the ghostly blows, as a sleek dark back sinks into the ripples. A v-shaped tail impales the surface, then disappears.

To someone standing on a coastal bluff or on the shifting shore, these spouts caused wonder, curiosity, even fear. The ocean was the realm of the sea monster, the great fish, or whale. In ancient Greek, the animal that created them was called *phallaina*. The origins of the word are obscure – perhaps from a root meaning blow or swell, or perhaps from phallus or *phallos*, for cork. (As the classicist William Wyatt noted, 'scholars are embarrassed about the word'.) Its origin may be obscure, but *phallaina* has survived in Latin as *balaena* and is retained in Spanish, *ballena*, in French, *baleine*, and in our own *baleen*. In Old English, it was *hwæl*, a word of Scandinavian origins. Our modern *whale* aspires to retain the soft echo of a blow. But the beast was also known as Cetus, the great fish, leviathan, the monster of the deep.

The shore-bound observer might have caught a glimpse, a flipper rising above the surface like a dark black sail, but only the seafarer, making the 'ocean paths' his home, came face-to-face with this spouting beast. To an anonymous English poet of the ninth century AD, the sea belonged to this whale:

> my heart leaps within me,
> my mind roams with the waves
> over the whale's domain, it wanders far and wide
> across the face of the earth, returns again to me
> eager and unsatisfied; the solitary bird screams,
> irresistible, urges the heart to the whale's way
> over the stretch of the seas.[1]

Viewed across the ocean, the whale's exhalation, condensed into a visible column of mist, was usually the first indication of a whale's presence. To some, this blow was a chimney. Early Arabian travellers saw minarets, or the sails of a distant ship.[2] If the spray was close enough, a colossal stench and a drizzle of briny mucous. The whale's spout fostered fear in early sailors: Norwegians believed that whales could spout enough water to swamp a boat. Others feared that inhaling the moist air could cause dizziness and fainting fits, possibly death; just a few droplets from the whale's toxic breath could raise a rash on human skin.[3]

Even Nearchus, the commander of Alexander the Great's fleet, feared the wrath of these sea monsters. He ordered his crew to blow trumpets and beat drums as his ships passed the huge beasts. When the whales approached the ships, the frightened oarsmen were hardly able to row.[4] Arabian sailors were on the lookout for an enormous fish, reported to be more than 90 metres long, 'that beateth the ship with its tail, and sinketh it'.[5]

Pliny the Elder described how the largest animal in the Bay of Biscay 'raises itself up like an enormous pillar, towering above the sails of the vessels and spouting a flood of water'. When a whale appeared off the coast of Ostia during the reign of Claudius, the Roman emperor ordered its capture. The whale was said to have sunk a boat with its spouts, before they could kill it. One of the first whales known to have a name was Porphyrios, or purple. It annoyed the city of Constantinople for fifty years, despite all attempts by the Emperor Justinian to capture it. When the whale stranded, purportedly while chasing dolphins, it was killed. It measured 30 cubits, or 15 metres. After a whale stranded along the Tiber during the reign of Septimius Severus, a model was made of it for a wild beast show, and 50 bears were driven into its mouth. Despite these exhibits, great whales do not appear in Roman art. Yet their smaller relatives, the dolphins, widely admired for their charm and speed, appear in almost every marine scene. The poet Oppian recognized these human-size cetaceans as the most godlike of all creatures.[6]

Cetus, the sea monster or whale, appears early in the Bible, populating the seas on the fourth day: 'And God said, Let the waters bring forth abundantly the moving creature that hath life . . . And God created great whales and every living creature that moveth, which the waters brought forth abundantly, after their kind' (Genesis I, 20–21).

It was not until modern translations of the Bible, such as the King James version quoted from above, that whales were distinguished from other large sea animals. For much of recorded history, there was little cosmological distinction between a sea monster, a cetacean or a great fish. Perhaps this is best exemplified in the Old Testament, where the whale appears in the form of leviathan. In the story of Job, God tells the persecuted man that He is beyond human measure.[7] Speaking from the whirlwind, God uses the leviathan as an example:

Canst thou draw out leviathan with an hook? or his tongue with a cord which thou lettest down? Canst thou put an hook into his nose? or bore his jaw through with a thorn? . . . Who can open the doors of his face? his teeth are terrible round about. His scales are his pride, shut up together as with a close seal . . . and his eyes are like the eyelids of the morning. Out of his mouth go burning lamps, and sparks of fire leap out. Out of his nostrils goeth smoke, as out of a seething pot or cauldron . . . Upon earth there is not his like who is made without fear.

Like God, the leviathan cannot be measured by man, or even understood by him. Yet despite its serpentine, draconic traits, the leviathan would become a synonym for cetacean.

Whale ribs, mandibles and scapulae were mounted in churches throughout the Middle Ages, providing osteological evidence of the leviathan. These *hierozoika* – items from the natural world held sacred for their mention in the Gospels – helped to sanction the power of the Church and local feudal lords,[8] for according to the whaling historian Klaus Barthelmess, the owner of these items had the 'world in his hands'. Church vaults might harbour ostrich eggs or stuffed crocodiles, but as Spenser wrote in *The Fairie Queene*, there was nothing on land that could compare with the whale and the other monsters of the sea:

> For all that here on earth we dreadfull hold
> Be but as bugs to fearen babes withall
> Compared to the creatures in the seas entrall[9]

By far, the Bible's most renowned whale is the 'great fish' that swallowed Jonah. When God sends him to Nineveh to save the city, Jonah tries to escape by sea, fleeing to the maritime country of Tarshish. God sends a great wind over the ocean, and to prevent the loss of the ship, Jonah is cast into the sea. 'Now the Lord had prepared a great fish to swallow up Jonah. And Jonah was in the belly of the fish three days and three nights'. From the deep, Jonah prays for forgiveness:

> The waters compassed me about, even to the soul: the depth closed me round about, the weeds were wrapped about my head . . . When my soul fainted within me I remembered the Lord: and my prayer came in unto thee, into thine holy temple.

Jonah's prayers were answered, and the fish vomited him out onto dry land. Following God's word this time, Jonah proceeded to Nineveh to save that wicked city. In the mosque at Nineveh, a whalebone commemorates Jonah's proclamation.

A 17th-century illustration of the story of Jonah, inscribed on the body of a whale.

The first edition of Martin Luther's exegesis of the Book of Jonah. Luther's translation of the Old Testament helped to establish the great fish as a whale.

Der Prophet Jona / ausgelegt durch Mart. Luth.

In the Greek translation, Jonah is swallowed by Cetus, a sea monster, which could be a whale, a shark, even an enormous cephalopod. By the New Testament, however, Jonah has spent 'three days and three nights in the whale's belly'.[10] According to Barthelmess, it was Martin Luther's exegesis of 1526 identifying the great fish as a whale that standardized the interpretation.

Luther's authority notwithstanding, religious scholars questioned the feasibility of whales for centuries. Could they swallow a person? 'The gullet of the *right whale* would not admit a man', the theologian Paul Haupt wrote in 1907, 'but the *sperm whale* or *cachalot* has a gullet quite large enough to enable him to swallow a man.'[11] There was anecdotal evidence that a man could survive in the belly of a shark or whale: some theologians cast the 'great fish' as a shark, using as support the tale of a sailor who fell overboard in the Mediterranean in 1758. A shark swallowed the sailor, and the captain fired on the monster, hitting it with cannon ball. The mariner was vomited out and rescued, having suffered little injury. In 1891 it was reported that a whale swallowed a man named James Bartley near the Falkland Islands. When the whale was captured the following day, Bartley was rescued by his fellow whalers, who restored him to consciousness. It took him three months to recover his reason.[12] Not surprisingly, marine historians refute the veracity of the story.

When whalers did get caught in the jaws of a toothed whale, they rarely escaped unscathed. The Nantucket captain Edmund Gardner recorded the aftermath of his run-in with a sperm whale in the Pacific in 1816:

> When on board, [I] found one tooth had entered my head breaking in my skull, another had pierced my hand, another had entered the upper part of my right arm, the fourth had entered my right shoulder . . . my jaw and five teeth were broken, tongue cut through, my left hand was pierced with a tooth . . . Twas favorable I retained my senses.[13]

Such danger encouraged tall stories. In one whaler's yarn, Bully Sprague, a harpooner with the strength to dart an iron straight through a whale, was swallowed by Timor Tom, an old grizzled sperm whale. Sitting on the whale's liver, with his legs swinging 'York fashion', Sprague used the light of a jellyfish to read the writing on the whale's stomach: Jonah. BC. 1683. Cutting a plug to console himself, Sprague noticed that Timor Tom wasn't used to tobacco. He escaped by packing the stomach with the rolled leaves: 'The whale began heavin' an' squirmin' real awful,

John Tabor's ride, an illustration of one of the many legends that arose from the whale fishery. From J. Ross Browne's *Etchings of a Whaling Cruise* (1846).

when, all at once, the stomach turned clean over with a flop like an earthquake, and I was shot out with about a cart-load of chawed squid that laid around the floor.'[14] The taller the tale, it was said, the better the chances of banishing sleep from the drowsy eyes of a late-night watch.

But why did God choose a whale? Haupt thought the giant sperm whale might have offered the fastest transport from Joppa, Jerusalem's seaport, to Alexendretta (now north-west Syria) en route to Nineveh.

A sperm-whale could easily swim from Joppa to Alexandretta in three days and three nights; the distance is only about 300 miles. The cachalot swims, as a rule, at a rate of from 3 to 7 miles an hour, and just under the surface of the water. If a sperm-whale swam seven miles an hour, it might rest more than nine hours a day and still cover the distance from Joppa to Alexandretta in three days and three nights, i.e., 72 hours. If Jonah had traveled overland on horseback, it would have taken more than two weeks . . . The gait of the horse of Palestine is a brisk walk; they hardly ever trot.[15]

St Methodius, a ninth-century missionary, didn't take the story so literally nor, perhaps, so drolly. He thought the whale signified time, 'which never stands still, but is always going on'. When Jonah was swallowed by the whale, he surrendered to the all-concealing earth, to time – 'his three days and as many nights in the whale's belly' were the past, the present and future.[16] After passing through time – or life – Jonah, like Christ in the New Testament, rose again. Beyond Earth, the past and the future are shed; there remains only the present and God.

The whale's colossal size fostered legends. St Brendan, an Irish monk born in AD 484, founded numerous abbeys and monasteries in Ireland and travelled widely around the British Isles and along the coast of Brittany. According to eleventh-century texts, late in life Brendan resolved to undertake a voyage in search of Tir na nÓg, translated as the Land of Promise, the Enchanted Isles and, by some, the Garden of Eden. He and seventeen fellow monks sailed the seas in a traditional Irish coracle, a boat constructed of willow and tanned ox hides, allowing the winds and the currents – God's will – to set their course.

Among his discoveries were the Isle of Fleas, the Isle of Mice and the Isle of Perpetual Day. This last island, along with reports of a huge crystal pillar in the midst of the sea, has been used as evidence that Brendan travelled far north and west of Ireland – with possible landfalls in Iceland and even North America. The whaling historian Stuart Frank, however, notes that most scholars 'concede only that Brendan visited Iona and Scotland, perhaps also the west coasts of England, Wales and Brittany'.[17]

At sea on Easter Sunday, Brendan and his monks landed on a barren island to say mass. As he prayed at the altar, the monks lit a fire to cook breakfast, and the earth stirred beneath them.

During St Brendan's search for the Enchanted Isles, he and his fellow monks stopped at a barren island to say mass. After they lit a fire, the island, actually a whale, awoke – tossing the monks into the sea.

When they reached their boat, the island swam away. The deceptive island was an enormous whale, Jasconius, who laboured 'night and day to put his tail in his mouth, but for greatness he may not'.[18] The whale disappeared over the horizon, with the remnants of the fire still burning. The monks later recovered their cauldron, which had come ashore near the Paradise of Birds. There a speaking bird declared that Brendan and his fellow voyagers must revisit the same islands during their journey. Jasconius offered his back again, for the monks to celebrate mass, but from then on they ate their meals cold.

On the voyage, there were good whales like Jasconius and bad whales. When the men were attacked by a sea monster, a 'terrible sea cat' with 'huge eyes and tusks rearing above the waves', a whale comes to the rescue, dragging the sea cat beneath the sea.[19] On the western edge of their voyage, the monks were pursued by a ferocious cetacean, spouting foam and threatening to overwhelm the boat. Brendan's prayers were answered in the form of a sea monster, which killed the whale after a long battle. Coming upon the dead whale the following day, the men cut into the carcass to provision their boat with meat.

Roman Catholic sailors, and probably many whalers, have long invoked Brendan before embarking on a voyage:

Shall I abandon, O King of Mysteries, the soft comforts of home? Shall I turn my back on my native land, and my face towards the sea? . . .

Shall I leave the prints of my knees on the sandy beach, a record of my final prayer in my native land? Shall I then suffer every kind of wound that the sea can inflict?

Shall I take my tiny coracle across the wide, sparkling ocean? O King of the Glorious Heaven, shall I go of my own choice upon the sea?

O Christ, will you help me on the wild waves?[20]

Fourteen centuries after his Atlantic voyage – when the cetaceans themselves required intervention – Brendan would become, by popular devotion, the patron saint of whales.

The island-size whale also appeared in *The Thousand and One Nights* during the seven voyages of Sinbad. On his first voyage, after squandering his parents' wealth and selling his household goods, Sinbad joined a company of merchants embarking upon the Persian Gulf en route to the East Indies. He recounted:

when the wind dropped suddenly, we found ourselves becalmed close to a small island like a green meadow,

During his first voyage, Sinbad also moored on a sleeping whale, which led to the loss of all his treasure.

which only rose slightly above the surface of the water. Our sails were furled, and the captain gave permission to all who wished to land for a while and amuse themselves. I was among the number, but when after strolling about for some time we lighted a fire and sat down to enjoy the repast which we had brought with us, we were startled by a sudden and violent trembling of the island, while at the same moment those left upon the ship set up an outcry bidding us come on board for our lives, since what we had taken for an island was nothing but the back of a sleeping whale. Those who were nearest to the boat threw themselves into it, others sprang into the sea, but before I could save myself the whale plunged suddenly into the depths of the ocean, leaving me clinging to a piece of the wood which we had brought to make our fire.

Sinbad, as always, was not to be outdone, and he recovered the goods lost after he was jettisoned by the whale. Trading them for 'sandal and aloes wood, camphor, nutmegs, cloves, pepper and ginger', he returned to his family in Baghdad a wealthy man.

Was this whale-island a figure of convergent literary evolution, or were they two branches of the story-telling tree from Islamic and European cultures? Cornelia Catlin Coulter traced the tale of landing on a fish to a section of the Talmud: 'we thought it was an island, descended, baked, and cooked upon it. When the back of the fish grew hot, it turned over, and had not the ship been so near we would have been drowned.' Coulter suggests that the story probably had its ultimate source in Indo-Persian folklore.[21]

To Brendan, Jasconius was a friendly whale, returning each year to offer his back to the monks, a cetacean island on which to celebrate mass. In *The Thousand and One Nights* the whale is one of the obstacles between Sinbad and wealth, his 'happy state'. Sinbad's view would dominate most of the shared history between men and whales.

Leviathan may slumber 'on the Norway foam' through Milton's *Paradise Lost*, where it 'seems a moving land',[22] but it is the swallow, or Jonah, motif that has followed the whale from antiquity into the twenty-first century. The Middle Ages, according to Borges, attributed the composition of two books to the Holy Spirit: the first was the Bible, of course, the second the whole world, 'whose creatures had locked up in them moral teachings'.[23] Bestiaries were compiled to explain these teachings. In Anglo-Saxon compilations, the whale might stand for the Devil, its maw becoming the gates of hell:

> When hunger comes upon him at sea
> And the grim creature wishes to have food,
> Then the sea-guardian opens up his mouth,
> His gaping lips: a pleasant smell comes forth
> From his insides, and by it other kinds

In an engraving after *The Last Judgement* of 1588 by Pieter Brueghel the Elder, the leviathan swallows the damned.

Of fishes of the sea become deceived
And, swift in swimming, go where the sweet smell
Emerges from him. Then they pass therein
In an unwary crowd, till the wide jaw
Is altogether filled; then suddenly
He shuts the grisly jaws together round
His booty; so it is for every man,
He who most often thinks about his life
Heedlessly in this transitory time,
Lets himself be deceived by the sweet smell,
The false desire . . .
When the malicious one, skilful in sin,
Has brought in those who used to call on him
To that safe place, that whirlpool of hot fire,
Loaded with guilt . . .

Then he snaps shut the grisly jaws on them,
Firmly together the strong doors of hell
After their death; and those who come therein
Have no return, escape, or parting ever,
Just as the fish who swim upon the sea
Can never turn away from the whale's grasp.[24]

In the twentieth century the whale's grasp was more likely a test of bravery or ingenuity. In Rudyard Kipling's *Just So Stories for Little Children*, a whale swallows a shipwrecked mariner. A 'person of infinite-resource-and-sagacity', the sailor uses his raft to construct a grate in the whale's throat, preventing the whale from consuming 'anything except very, very small fish; and that is the reason', Kipling explains, 'why whales nowadays never eat men or boys or little girls'.[25] Tell that to Walt Disney. In his *Pinocchio*, the puppet becomes a real boy by escaping from the belly of the evil whale Monstro.

The ultimate swallow motif, perhaps, is the leviathan of Thomas Hobbes. For Hobbes, leviathan is the 'mortal god', the commonwealth, with reward and punishment its nerves, 'wealth and riches' its strength, and 'sedition, sickness; and civil war, death'.[26] For George Orwell, we are all in the whale: 'Get inside the whale – or rather, admit you are inside the whale (for you *are*, of course). Give yourself over to the world-process.' For those who didn't fight it, Orwell noted, the whale's belly is an enviable place, 'a womb big enough for an adult. There you are, in the dark, cushioned space that exactly fits you, with yards of blubber between yourself and reality, able to keep up an attitude of the completest indifference, no matter *what* happens.'[27] Which is not to say it's easy – from Georg Büchner to Tom Waits, we find suffering in the commonwealth:

Cetus, the whale constellation, from Sidney Hall's hand-coloured etching for Jehoshaphat Aspin's *A Familiar Treatise on Astronomy* (1825).

Starving in the belly
Starving in the belly of a whale ...
Tell me who gives a good gaddamn
You'll never get out alive[28]

The disappearance of the human into a monstrous belly – whether in the physical form of a cetacean or the metaphorical state – is an essential component of our vision of the whale.

Whale, cetus, leviathan or great fish – it is difficult to determine where sea monsters end and whales begin; perhaps it is a fool's errand, since for much of recorded history there was no cosmological distinction between the two. European depictions of whales from the sixteenth century to the nineteenth form a cetacean hall of mirrors: many depictions were reflections of the past – unchecked by empirical observation. An occasional image, rendered accurately from a whale stranding, did enter the canon, but in medieval and early modern times people did not investigate the reason: they interpreted the meaning of stranding within

Sebastian Münster's famous *Cosmographie Universelle*, helped to propagate the idea of the existence of sea monsters. At upper-left barrels are thrown overboard, believed to be a handy method of distracting monsters – in this case a spouting whale – from attacking the vessel.

the framework of God's plan for human salvation – a whale leaving its watery element was often interpreted as an evil omen, a sign of God's displeasure.[29]

Olaus Magnus's *Carta marina*, a large map of Scandinavia, is one of the earliest and finest depictions of sea life – illustrating the fine line between monsters and whales. Magnus, a Swedish archbishop and historian, was long considered an authority on Scandinavian history, and after his marine map was published in 1539 his images of whales appeared and reappeared for centuries. (One striking illustration, a spouting fish with claws, may have been the result of a mistranslation between Swedish and Latin, the cleric mistaking the word *fin* for claws. The mistake, if that's what it was, survived until the nineteenth century.)

The Swiss naturalist and physician Conrad Gesner borrowed heavily from Magnus in compiling his *Historiae animalium*, which he began in 1551, one of the earliest works of modern zoology. A ground-breaking biologist, Gesner was nevertheless an extremely credulous one. His compendium – intended to

Conrad Gesner's *Historiae Animalium* (1551–8) is one of the earliest illustrated compendiums to include whales. Gesner was a great naturalist, though a credulous one. In addition to one of the earliest depictions of flensing, men are shown moored on a whale's back and using barrels and music to fend off an attack.

Ist ein grosser Wallfisch/welchen die Einwohner der Insel Fare genannt Fischfresser/auß dem ungestümen Meer in den Sand hinauß geworffen/und mit einem grossen eysnen Hacken an das Land herauß gezogen/mit Achsen und Beilen zu Stück hauen/und unter sich selber theilen.

Die vierdte.

Ist ein Turckwall mit Sand überstreuet/auff welchem die Schiffleut / als auff einer kleinen Insel angelehnet kochen/das Schiff daran geheftet haben / also aber manchesmahl in grosse Gefahr kommen/wie oben erwehnet worden.

Die fünffte.

harbour everything known about every animal, including those observed, hinted at or simply imagined – reinforced a belief in mythical spouting monsters that would survive in illustrated histories for centuries.[30] Yet, in his second edition Gesner depicted one of the earliest known images of blubber being removed from a whale. Anchored to the shore, the whale with

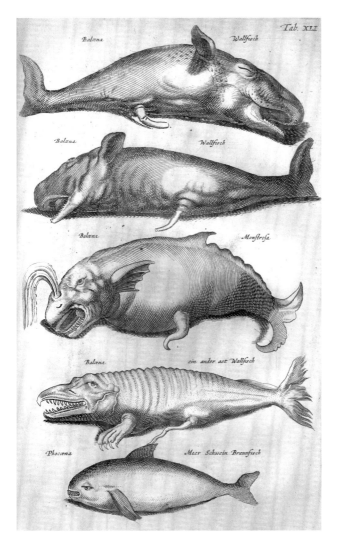

Into the 17th century, images of stranded whales populated natural history books, along with sea monsters such as the 'Montrosa' in the centre of this Dutch etching of 1660.

four right teats and a pair of spout stalks was probably not drawn from life.

But even when a whale was at hand, and an artist could depict the animal in front of him, the stock image – the fishlike vertical dorsal tail, scaled fins and pointed teeth – was often used to advertise a whale on exhibition. The whale was an icon, not an animal that could be observed. Frank notes: 'Misshapen images and ill-informed descriptions of whales created an unfounded multiplicity of variant species that piled up one upon another, unchecked by empirical corroboration.'[31]

An image from a natural history of 1660 throws light – in clean-burning whale oil – on the seventeenth-century perception of whales, a combination of observation, speculation and derivation from medieval creatures. Two of the cetaceans are sperm whales, copied from images of strandings along the Dutch shore; one is a harbour porpoise; and Balaena and Monstrosa are sea monsters, under the influence of Magnus. Frequent depictions reinforced the belief in the existence of such creatures.[32]

As Europe emerged from the Middle Ages, what was a whale? No matter how grotesque or fanciful the monster, it was the spout – the briny white exhalation – that often signified a cetacean. Like the whale itself, this breath could be perceived on a geographical scale. According to Borges, the German astronomer Johann Kepler debated with the English mystic Robert Fludd over which of them had first conceived of the notion of the earth as a living monster, 'whose whalelike breathing, changing with sleep and wakefulness, produces the ebb and flow of the sea'.[33] It was along this shifting edge of the ocean that humans first encountered whales.

2 The Invention of Whaling

A whale, disoriented, sick or wounded, perhaps just old, can find itself in shallow waters. Its first understanding of the burden of gravity ashore is also its last. In the ocean, some whales are positively buoyant, floating to the surface when at rest; others remain neutral, able to dive and surface with ease. But no cetacean can survive long on land, where its enormous body collapses on the rocks or sand. As the tide goes out, a hill of meat rises on the water's edge, a black flipper pointing to the sky.

The first humans to eat whale were probably scavengers removing the blubber, meat and perhaps baleen from stranded whales. If they were lucky, there was enough meat to supply an entire village or even to trade with nearby tribes.

This taste for whale drew hunters to the sea in search of fresh cetacean, and the hunting of whales arose independently throughout the globe. In antiquity, sperm whales were hunted in the Indian Ocean from the shores of Zanzibar; right whales were killed along their breeding grounds off the coast of Florida; bowheads were chased on the Arctic shores of Siberia; fin whales, humpbacks and grey whales were killed with poison darts in the North Pacific.[1] The earliest depictions of whaling are Neolithic petroglyphs. A sandstone wall in southern Korea, which may date back to 6000 BC, bears an image of a boatload of men tethered to a whale. Whale carvings from 2000 BC have been found

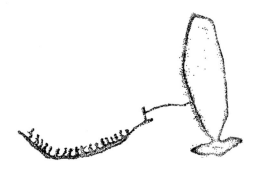

One of the earliest images of whaling, a Neolithic wall drawing at Bangu-Dae, South Korea, depicts a whale harpooned by a boatload of men.

in the rock of Rødøy, an island off the northern Norwegian coast.

Although early techniques of capturing whales included barbed darts and setting traps in bays, it was the development of the harpoon that enabled humans to exploit these large aquatic animals. The oldest of these barbed spears date back 40,000 years to East Africa, where they were used to hunt the hippopotamus.[2] Unlike an arrow or dart, the harpoon head is designed to remain within the wound, enabling the quarry to be tethered by a line, essential to hunting animals in the three dimensions of the ocean. A whale's reaction to an attack on the surface was often to sound, or dive. A barb with a high retention factor – sometimes with a movable head – permitted the harpoon to hold fast to a sounding whale.[3] It was an especially attractive weapon because it required little manpower at the other end of the line – a float, a wooden drogue or even the boat of the hunters could be used to tire the whale and track it until death.

In the ice-rimed north, it was the bowhead whale, *Balaena mysticetus*, with an insulating layer of blubber 50 centimetres thick and a head big enough to burst through solid ice, that provided sustenance for early whaling cultures. The blue whale may be the largest animal on the planet, but the bowhead has the biggest mouth – with 3-metre baleen plates and a tongue 5 metres long and 3 metres wide. Despite the enormous gulp, it feeds mostly on copepods; a thousand of these minute crustaceans can fit on a teaspoon.

Bowheads are among the longest-lived animals: Naluataliq, a white-tailed bowhead, has been sited off Baffin Island for more than a hundred years. In 1995 a crew of Iñupiat whalers from Wainwright, Alaska, found two stone harpoon blades in the blubber of a whale they were butchering. Stone points had not been used for more than a century – not since commercial whalers brought metal tools to the Arctic and traded them to the natives. Bowheads are also among the slowest to reach adulthood; females do not reach sexual maturity until their late teens

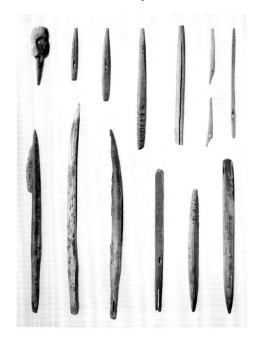

In the North Pacific, early harpoon points were often fashioned from bone.

or mid-twenties (by that age a typical Inuit woman might be nursing her third child).[4] Early hunters targeted these immature animals. Ninety-seven per cent of the bowheads uncovered in the bone middens of Somerset Island, now part of Nunavut in the Canadian Arctic, were sub-adults less than 10 metres long. The small skulls and mandibles of bowhead calves are often found in Alaskan ruins. Yet if a young bowhead made it to adulthood, it could easily outlive the whaler who had tried to kill it as a calf – and then bury his son and his grandson as well.

To the hunters in the Arctic, all sea mammals came from the south, where the souls of whales they killed would return to be reborn.[5] The current understanding of bowhead whale migrations reflects this ancient belief: bowheads travel south in winter, never straying far from the marginal ice zone. Calves are born during this spring migration, while the whales are moving through a long corridor in the polar ice – along stress cracks, polynyas (areas of the ocean that remain open through winter) and shore leads – into the Beaufort or Chukchi Seas.

At the heart of the Inuit relationship with whales, seals and walruses was Sedna, the goddess of marine mammals and the sea. (The use of the term 'Inuit' or 'Eskimo' for the native peoples of Chukotka, northern Alaska, Canada and Greenland continues to be debated. I have followed the style of the Arctic specialists in the *Encyclopedia of Marine Mammals* and use Inuit to describe these cultures.) Known by many names – Nuliajuk, the poor wife; Arna kapfaluk, the big woman; and Takanapak saluk, the terrible one down there – Sedna was a primal force of nature throughout the Arctic. In one version of her story, recorded on Baffin Island in 1888, Sedna is raised by her father on a solitary shore. Beautiful and proud, she turns down all the Inuit youths who come to court her. One day a seabird entices her to accompany him to the land of the birds: 'My fellows, the fulmars, shall bring you all your heart may desire; their feathers shall clothe you, your lamp will always be filled with oil, your pot with meat.'

Sedna consents, but after a long hard journey she finds that she was deceived. Her new home is covered in draughty fish skins, and her bed is rough walrus hide. She regrets her earlier refusals of the Inuit youths and calls on her father: 'O come and take me back home. Aja.' After a year has passed, the father comes to visit Sedna.

His daughter greeted him joyfully and besought him to take her home. The father hearing of the outrages wrought upon his daughter determined upon revenge. He killed the fulmar, took Sedna into his boat, and they quickly left the country which had brought so much sorrow to Sedna. When the other fulmars came home and found their companion dead and his wife gone, they all flew away in search of the fugitives. They were very sad over the death of their poor murdered comrade and continue to mourn and cry until this day.

Having flown a short distance they discerned the boat and stirred up a heavy storm. The sea rose in immense waves and threatened the pair with destruction. In this mortal peril the father determined to offer Sedna to the birds and flung her overboard. She clung to the edge of the boat with a death grip. The cruel father then took a knife and cut off the first joints of her fingers. Falling into the sea they were transformed into whales, the nails turning into whalebone. Sedna holding onto the boat more tightly, the second finger joints fell under the sharp knife and swam away as seals; when the father cut off the stumps they became ground seals. Meantime the storm subsided, for the fulmars thought Sedna was drowned. The father then allowed her to come into the boat again. But from that time she cherished a deadly hatred against him and swore bitter revenge. After they got ashore, she called her dogs and let them gnaw off the feet and hands of her father while he was asleep. Upon this he cursed himself, his daughter, and the dogs which had maimed him; whereupon the earth opened and swallowed the hut, the father, the daughter, and the dogs.[6]

Understandably, Sedna was feared and revered, and in times of need, shamans would visit her, combing her long hair to appease her. When the Danish explorer Knud Rasmussen asked an Inuit if he really believed in Nuliajuk, or Sedna, the hunter responded: 'We don't believe, we only fear. And most of all we fear Nuliajuk.'[7]

A whale-bone house on Somerset Island, Nunavut. Around AD 800, the Thule people expanded the hunt for bowheads into open water. They consumed the blubber and meat and lived within the whale, in houses constructed of ribs and mandibles.

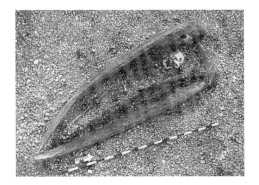

The grave of an Inuit whaler, framed by whale mandibles on St Lawrence Island, Canada, about AD 850.

Archaeological evidence indicates that whaling cultures arose about 2,000 years ago along the Bering and Chukchi seas. The Birnik culture had begun hunting whales by AD 400, but it was the Thule culture, which arose in north Alaska about AD 800, that expanded the hunt for bowheads into open water. Eating blubber and living within the whale – they used ribs and mandibles for building huts – the Thule became the dominant culture in the Arctic, dispersing into the Bering Sea and east to Greenland as they followed the bowhead migration route.

On a cetacean diet, societies grew in size and became more aggressive. With whaling came warfare – the discipline and structure of the whaling crew provided a framework in which inter-societal wars could thrive.[8] The whaler-warriors, emboldened in their armour of walrus ivory and sealskin, rose in status. Although the Old Bering Sea cultures generally did not bother with burials, Thule whalers were interred in whalebone graves: whale mandibles and scapulae were used to frame the corpse, perhaps to protect the whaler on his journey after death, a funereal swallow motif.

The Thule whale hunt permanently changed the north. Many of the culture's rituals and hunting techniques continued in the Arctic and the Pacific Northwest for a thousand years. And the ecological effects of the hunt are still being discovered. In 2004 the Canadian geologist Marianne Douglas and her colleagues found evidence that the nutrient-rich by-products of the whale hunt had leached into a freshwater pond near an 800-year-old settlement. Not only did the bowhead hunt affect these ponds 1,000 years ago, but algal blooms are still evident today, 400 years after the settlement was abandoned.[9]

Whalers depended on local resources, or trade, to make their tools. In the Pacific Northwest, the harpoon head, often made of elk horn, was bound to the shaft with sea-lion sinew. Whalers glued mussel-shell blades into the barbs with spruce gum.[10] In the Arctic, where trees were rare, harpoon shafts were fashioned from driftwood or traded up the coast. The bladders of narwhals, walruses and seals were used as floats to the harpoon. Sometimes entire seals, skinned through the mouth with all orifices and wounds sewn shut, were used as drogues. Inflated through a bone tube, each seal float created a drag of about 100 kilograms, exhausting the whale and reducing its chance of escape.

Approaching a bowhead, the captain assessed the temper of the whale. In Nunavut, the blowholes of docile whales lay flat on the sea's surface, whereas the holes of aggressive whales rose to a point – these whales were deemed too dangerous to approach. Sleeping whales were also avoided – the thrashing of their flukes when they awoke could injure the hunters. If a whale's blow sounded like the crack of breaking ice, it was considered a warning to the crew, who would abandon the chase.[11]

Around the Bering Strait, whale was an essential form of sustenance. The skin, often eaten raw as *maqtaq*, was rich in vitamin C, hard to come by during long northern winters. The meat provided protein. Whale and seal oil were also consumed throughout the region. Captain George Vancouver wrote in his journal in August 1793, while visiting the Tlingit of the Pacific Northwest:

> The chiefs remained on board the greater part of the forenoon, and became very sociable . . . Bread & molasses were the greatest treat we could give these people; the chiefs ate heartily of it, and distributed some amongst their particular friends in the canoes alongside. In return for this delicious repast, they took much pains to recommend to us some of their whale oil, which stunk most intolerably. This was brought into the cabin in a bladder, out of which a spoonful was very carefully poured by the chief, who extolled its superior qualities, and gave us to understand that, as a delicacy, it was quite equal to our treacle; and it was not without much difficulty, that I was able to excuse myself from partaking of their nauseious meal, which they seemed to relish in the highest degree; and finished it with a large glass of rum, a luxury to which they seemed by no means strangers.[12]

After the whale was killed, the community was suddenly rich. 'Wealth begat leisure', Stefani Paine notes, 'and the time to create and refine harpoon heads of various configuration and

Eskimo string figures were used to capture the sun before it disappeared for the winter. This figure represents a stranded whale and a hungry fox. When the thumb and index fingers are moved, the fox is chased away.

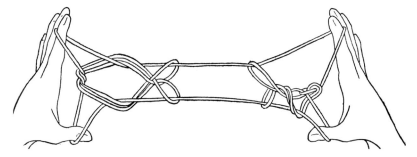

materials, some for whales, some for seals, and gadgets of all kinds – swivels for line, plugs for floats, snow picks, combs and goggles.'[13] The long baleen strips were fashioned into toboggans, and jawbones and whale ribs were used as runners for sleds.[14] Houses were built of whale bones; in Siberia, ribs formed arches above a stone wall, the long heavy jawbones sustaining the weight of the structure. Walrus hides were laid over the bones and lashed to the whale vertebrae.[15] The Inuit could spend the winter riding on whales.

The earliest kayaks, *baidarkas* in Russian, had whale-bone frames covered in sealskin. For modern kayakers used to a rigid hull, the give in the skin might seem unsettling at first. Joseph Lubischer described the flexibility of hunting from a 'living' vessel:

> I think it enlightening to try and crawl inside the mind and soul of an early master baidarka builder. How did he see and feel his task? All builders, sooner or later, generate a model – an ideal or visualization – of what they are striving for in order to help with the work. Dyson commented that 'the baidarka, of driftwood, whalebone, and sea lion skin, was entirely a creature of the sea'. . . Taking whales, sea lions, sea dogs, sea horses, and sea otters as his examples, he sought to emulate their characteristics in the floating craft. These living creatures in a living sea pointed towards a living vessel. A living vessel that breathed air in and out of the gap between the paddler and skin as its ribs worked the troughs and peaks of the sea. A living vessel whose skin caressed the shape of the waves.[16]

The hunt for bowheads and grey whales changed societies throughout the Arctic and North Pacific. With a steady supply of

An early 18th-century depiction of subsistence whaling off the Greenland coast by the Norwegian missionary Hans Egede.

food, permanent villages were established and flourished.[17] Cooperation in the hunt gave an advantage to larger groups. And whalers, skilled in the techniques of hunting and imitative magic required to attract whales, were revered, part of an elite hierarchy in many groups. A network of trade flourished among the settlements.

When Captain James Cook arrived in the Pacific Northwest in the 1780s he noted that the whole method of the whale fishery was captured in the hats worn by the whaling chiefs. Woven by the coastal Nootka, now known as the Nuu-chah-nulth, of Vancouver Island, the hats were made of spruce root, surf grass and fur. The caps confirmed the status of the whaling chief, keeping him dry while helping to establish contact with the animal world. A few decades later, when Meriwether Lewis and William Clark travelled along the Columbia River, they were impressed by these same bulb-topped hats, worn by local chiefs, with 'faint representations of the whales, the Canoes, and the harpooners Strikeing them'. These maritime caps, worn far from the sea, provided evidence of the trade network and of inter-tribal gifts, marriage and even raids.[18]

In her study of whaling rituals, the American anthropologist Margaret Lantis suggested that a whale-hunting cult extended from Kamchatka to Hudson Bay, and from Point Barrow, Alaska, to the coast of Washington State. She noted that the cult perhaps even extended from Japan to Greenland.[19] In fact, the boundaries might be said to have ranged beyond mere geography: for some hunters, it was not until the whale surfaced in a dream that the hunt began. Just as he needed the skills to fashion bone harpoons and skin boats, a successful whaler had to bind the dream state to his waking life.

For many cultures, purity was also essential. It was taboo for a Nuu-chah-nulth whaler to sleep with his wife for a month before the hunt. If any member of the crew committed adultery, the hunt would fail, and the captain would blame him for the loss. At home, the hunter's wife was to remain inactive during his absence, with the door open to welcome the whale. If a stranger entered the home, the hunt would be unsuccessful. Women also played an important role in enticing strandings.

Nuu-chah-nulth whale ceremony: a Nootka Indian taking a ceremonial bath before a whale hunt, photographed by Edward Curtis *c.* 1910.

Nuu-chah-nulth shamans built secluded purifying houses, where they placed pieces of their wife's excrement. The faeces turned into spirits, bringing whales to the beach.[20]

The Aleut whale hunter rubbed human fat or menstrual secretion on the tips of his spears. Makah whalers of the Olympic Peninsula, in present-day Washington State, imitated their grey whale quarry before each hunt, diving deep into the water and staying down as long as possible. Each time they surfaced, the hunter would spout a mouthful of water towards the centre of the lake, trying to sound like a whale.[21] The most determined divers were reported to surface with blood trickling from their ears.

Northern hunters also used songs and amulets to increase their chances of killing and retrieving whales. The harpoon-rests along the gunwales of boats were adorned with images of animals, often bears or seals, designed to comfort the whales, not frighten them off.

There was real danger in breaking the taboos, or in being unprepared. According to the ethnologist Philip Drucker,

> The whale might turn toward the canoe, smashing it to bits in one of his blind rushes; a crewman might be badly injured by a blow from a float or the rigid line, or even be caught in a bight and dragged to his death. It was mainly for this moment that the whaler and his crew practiced long drill sessions and carried out arduous rituals of ceremonial purification to forestall any mishaps.[22]

The Aleut and the Nuu-chah-nulth used the spirits of the dead to bring whales ashore.[23] Human skeletons and corpses could communicate with whales: shamans employed skulls during ritual baths to attract dead whales to shore, and a whaler might carry a skeleton on his back during ceremonial bathing.[24] Occasionally, a corpse was propped up, holding a line attached to a whale effigy. The whaler might pray directly to his quarry:

Whale, I want you to come near me,
so that I will get hold of your heart and deceive it,
so that I will have strong legs and not be trembling
and excited when the whale comes and I spear him.
Whale, you must not run out to sea when I spear you.
Whale, if I spear you, I want my spear to strike your heart.
Harpoon, when I use you, I want you to go to the heart of the
    whale.
Whale, when I spear at you and miss you,
I want you to take hold of my spear with your hands.
Whale, do not break my canoe, for I am going to do good to
    you.
I am going to put eagle-down and cedar bark in your back.[25]

After harpooning a whale, the Aleut hunter returned to a secluded house, where he remained for three days without food and water. Here, he imitated the sighs and groans of the injured whale, in an effort to cause it to die and strand. Emerging from seclusion on the fourth day, the hunter searched for the dead animal. If the whale failed to appear, the hunter repeated the seclusion ritual.[26]

In some cultures, poison was used to hasten death. Kodiak Island whalers laced their lances with aconite, a poison derived from the dried root of monkshood, a plant associated with witchcraft in medieval Europe. It took about three days for the poison to kill the whale; the hunters waited for the carcass to drift ashore, hoping that they would not lose their quarry to the sea or, worse, to their neighbours.

The Aleut hunted right whales with lances tipped with aconite poison from the dried root of the monkshood plant.

After the whale was killed, the biggest challenge was the tiresome chore of towing the enormous quarry ashore. Nuu-chah-nulth whalers employed charms to coax the whale ashore; some tied hummingbirds to the line, others turtles. Whaling chants were passed down through the generations – and sometimes captured, as if they were drift whales, by ethnologists in an effort called salvage ethnology. This Makah prayer was recorded by Edward Curtis:

Whale, turn toward the fine beach of Yahksis,
and you will be proud to see
the young men come down on the fine sandy beach
of my village at Yahksis to see you;
and the young men will say to one another:
'What a great whale he is! What a fat whale he is!
What a strong whale he is!' And you, whale, will be proud

of all that you will hear them say of your greatness . . .
young men will cover your great body
with bluebill duck feathers, and with the down
of the great eagle, the chief of all birds;
for this is what you are wishing,
and this is what you are trying to find
from one end of the world to the other.[27]

A spirit of camaraderie and praise is also evident in a chant from the south-west coast of Alaska:

Come, oh sea lord, chief of the waters. We are your
    friends!
We wish you well. We bring you to a place to do you great
    honor.
You are dying, but your death will not be forgotten.
We will strip your bones of flesh, but we will send them
    back to the sea
that you may live again, so fear not.
Let us lead you to the Kaniagmiut, people who admire
    you,
great lord of the ocean![28]

The belief in regeneration – that whales were sent back to the sea and later returned – was essential to the rituals of many cultures. In the north, as soon as the whale was hauled out and before the butchering began, it was presented with a ceremonial 'drink' of freshwater to placate its spirit.[29] Following a successful hunt, communities from Kamchatka to Vancouver Island had a period of ritual mourning of about three days, as long as that for a man.[30] Dances and feasts often ended the ritual. On Cape Prince of Wales, the wife and children of the whaling captain danced inside a circle of whale ribs upon receiving the news of a successful hunt. A ceremonial fire was built to cook a piece of the fluke.[31] On St Lawrence Island, a small figure of a whale was painted on the right side of the umiak.[32] A reckless kill or a whale that was not shared among the community could, it was thought, result in the loss of future whales.

In this tradition, whalers, shamans and their wives employed imitative magic to capture whales: they were often expected to suffer just as their prey did. It would take a small group of hunters on a hilly temperate coastline to break this tradition, changing the relationship between humans and whales forever. Or at least these Europeans would get the credit, and later the blame.

A walrus-ivory baton used to accompany ritual dancing in Port Clarence, Alaska. Down feathers represent the whale's spout.

3   The Royal Fish

As whaling spread around the Arctic, the Celts and the Romans, and later the Moors, conquered much of Europe, filling the continent with variations on a single Indo-European linguistic theme. But on the northern edge of the Iberian peninsula, the Basques, pastoralists and fishermen, held firm to their native Euskara, a language so foreign to other Europeans that one cleric wrote: 'the Basques speak among themselves in a tongue that they say they understand but I frankly do not believe it.'[1]

Yet the Europeans did have faith in one thing Basque – the ability to hunt whales. The word *harpoon* comes from *arpoi*, 'to take quickly' in Euskara. The barbed dart with the high retention factor may have been fast, but it was also gruesome: the Basques developed the implements and the techniques that would be followed by whalers for centuries. In *Moby-Dick*, when Ishmael arrives at the Spouter Inn in New Bedford, he spies a Yankee harpoon that could just as well have been found on the bow of a Basque whaleboat: 'You shuddered as you gazed, and wondered what monstrous cannibal and savage could ever have gone a death-harvesting with such a hacking, horrifying implement.'[2]

Other Europeans chased whales – the Vikings were exporting meat and ivory in the eighth century – but the Basques were the first to develop an industry that would stretch across an entire ocean – by depleting one region in the Atlantic and then sailing

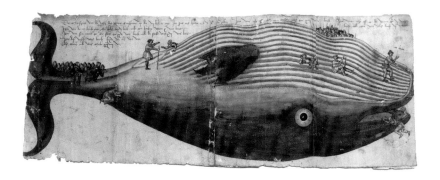

A rare stranding of a fin whale in Holland in 1547 piqued the curiosity of the monks of the local abbey.

on to another. In the eleventh and twelfth centuries, if you wanted whale oil or meat, you traded with the Basques. With commerce came a significant shift in the human perspective on whales.[3] Basque pastoralists, who maintained flocks in the mountains of Navarra, began to move to the fishing villages along the Bay of Biscay. They did not move for subsistence but to sell the products of the North Atlantic right whale, *Eubalaena glacialis*, the first commercial whale. In fact, some scientists have proposed *euskariensis* as the proper species epithet, since the whale was long known by its association with Basque whalers. In English, however, it has always been the *right* whale to hunt – a slow coastal swimmer that floated to the surface after it was killed. Averaging about 13 to 16 metres in length, right whales border on the rotund – the girth of a healthy adult may exceed 60 per cent of its total body length.[4]

Calves are about 5 metres in length and weigh about 1,000 kilograms at birth, and they grow fast, doubling in length by the time they are weaned, only one year after they are born. (Females usually give birth once every three years – one year for gestation, one for nursing and a third to replenish energy stores.)[5] Unlike the bowhead, whose enormous head is dark and sleek, the right whale has callosities on its bonnet, the hourglass-shaped upper jaw. A callosity is a mass of roughened skin with thousands of white cyamids, or whale lice, gathered around the patches of skin like a drift of deep-packed snow. Descending from the inside of this upper jaw are approximately 400 slabs of black baleen, a sieve designed for straining small crustaceans such as copepods.

All along the coast of the Bay of Biscay, lookouts were posted in *vigìas* or stone towers to look for this enormous planktivore. When the bushy blow of a right whale was spotted, a call rang out, sometimes in code to mask the finding from other hunters. In this winter nursery, the mothers might be difficult to spot from shore, but a newborn, perhaps bobbing playfully above the waterline, could easily be seen from more than a kilometre away.

When the cry was heard from the *vigìa*, six oarsmen, the captain and a harpooner rushed to attack. On the bow of the *chalupa*, the 8-metre boat employed in the hunt, the harpooner turned and thrust the barbed blade of iron deep into the side of the whale. When the injured creature submerged, the whaleboat followed on the surface, a buoyant drag on the dying animal. A whaler was poised with a lance in the *chalupa* above, ready to strike as soon as the whale broke the surface to breathe. After death, the bouyant carcass, rich in oil, was towed back to shore.

Hans Bols's 1582 engraving is the earliest European image of commercial whaling. Although the fishery was focused on right whales, the cetaceans are probably derived from contemporary illustrations of stranded sperm whales. The naked whalers may represent Native Americans.

Whales were central to medieval Basque culture and economy. The coats of arms of Biarritz, Hendaye and Motrico depict whales and whaleboats.

As a Basque whaler stood in the *vigía*, he looked out on an untapped resource, an ocean of ghostly blows and dark flukes. At his back, a steady flow of traders travelled from north of the Pyrenees to the Iberian peninsula, and on to Africa. In such a prime location – the well-travelled trail to Santiago de Compostela, one of the principal pilgrimage sites in Europe, runs though the region – Basques found a 'ready market for almost the entire carcass' of the right whales they brought ashore.[6] Unlike Inuit and Norwegian subsistence hunters, the Basques whaled for profit. They sold oil for light, lubrication and soap; baleen for whips and fishing rods; bones for posts and gateways; and skin for shoes. Whale meat was an essential part of the Roman Catholic diet on Fridays and during Lent, when red meat was forbidden. On such days, only the flesh from animals that lived in water could be consumed. For the rich, this included whale tongue, a delicacy in the Middle Ages. The poor consumed *craspois*, or *lard de carême* – 'Lent butter', whale meat salt-cured like bacon. Like fatback or lard, it was often cooked with peas.[7]

The transition from subsistence to commercial use meant that the hunters and consumers were often unconnected to the ecosystems of the whaling grounds. Unlike the Inuit, who had elaborate rituals and a strong dependence on the survival of the species, whalers intent on profit had no such motivation. The Spanish historian Alex Aguilar estimates that the Basques removed as many as 40,000 right whales from the Atlantic between 1530 and 1610. They were, according to the whaling historian Richard Ellis, 'the advance guard of what would eventually become an all-out war on whales'.[8] They could not gather this many whales at home, of course – by the 1600s the bushy v-shaped blows of the right whale were becoming rare around the Bay of Biscay. Whalers from the coastal communities of Fuenterrabia, Hendaye and Biarritz would soon take their battles to the far shores of the Atlantic.

Although the Basques garner much of the credit for the development of commercial whaling, the Vikings had probably whaled for centuries before the Bay of Biscay became a renowned hunting ground. There is a long history of whale consumption in Scandinavia and Iceland. In fact, the Basques may have hired Norwegians to teach them to whale at the start of commercial exploitation. Such work for hire expanded whaling throughout the globe. When the Dutch and English started whaling, they hired Basques. The Shinnecock and other Native Americans were employed when colonists arrived on their shore.

In the Icelandic *Saga of Grettir the Strong* from the fourteenth century, two chiefs claim a large fin whale that has stranded on their shore.

Hard were the blows which were dealt at Rifsker;
No weapons they had but the steaks of the whale.
They belaboured each other with rotten blubber,
Unseemly methinks is such warfare for men.[9]

To avoid such unseemly battles, laws were written to establish ownership of stranded whales. According to Old Norse law, a harpooned whale driven ashore was divided equally between the landowner and the hunter. A dead whale found at sea was to be divided between the harpooner, if he had witnesses to his attack, and whoever retrieved the whale.[10] In Denmark, all stranded whales were royal fish, belonging to the king, since he owned the shore. But the person who discovered the whale was permitted a share – as much as he could carry if he were on foot, a larger amount if riding and a ship's charge if at sea. The king always kept the greater part of the bone and meat. As far back as the fourteenth century, English and Scottish royalty had similar prerogatives over whales stranded or hunted along their coasts. Whales are still 'Fishes Royal' in the United Kingdom, although now for the benefit of science rather than the consumption of kings.[11]

Church records reveal that whalebone even funded the Crusades. Since Greenland had no currency in the Middle Ages, the Crusade tax was levied in sealskin, cattle hide and baleen. One of the most important texts from this region is the *King's*

The Franks Casket is an 8th-century whale-bone box from northern England. The inscription in Old English on the front describes its cetaceous origin: 'The King of terror became sad when he swam onto the shingle.'

Mirror, a thirteenth-century Norse work in the form of a dialogue between father and son. In the section on Iceland and Greenland, 21 whales are named and described – from their behaviour to the edibility of their meat and protected status. As in the Basque country, the right whale was recognized as a desirable prize:

> People say it does not eat any food except darkness and the rain which falls on the sea. And when it is caught and its intestines opened, nothing unclean is found in its stomach as would be in other fish that eat food, because its stomach is clean and empty. It cannot open its mouth easily, because the baleen that grows there rises up in the mouth when it is opened, and often causes its death because it cannot shut its mouth. It does no harm to ships: it has no teeth, and is a fat fish and edible.[12]

In northern Europe, the procurement of whale meat was not limited to strandings. Because of its visits to bays and shoreline, the 9-metre minke, the smallest baleen whale, has been caught for food since antiquity. Villagers trapped minkes with herring nets suspended across the narrow fjords of Norway, then shot them with arrows attached to wooden floats. The tip of the *dödspiler*, or death arrow, was covered with bacillus – preferably from the inflamed sore of a dead whale or some other rotten meat – causing septicaemia in the small whale. Within 36 hours, the bacteria would weaken the whale enough to permit an easy kill with a harpoon. The whale meat was still edible, except around the wound.[13]

Improvements in living standards in the sixteenth century increased the demand for illuminants and soaps. Vegetable oil was expensive, but artificial light was essential for a craftsman to

In Europe, whale shoulder-blades (c. 1 metre in length) were sometimes used as street signs for inns and other businesses. Here the right shoulder-blade of a bowhead advertises an inn in north Germany.

remain productive through the long, dark winters. Worse, crop failures could cause prices to spike beyond his means. Whale oil provided a cheap, clean-burning alternative, and its source was not subject to droughts, frosts or floods.

As right-whale populations declined in Europe, the Basques spread out across the Atlantic in search of prey. In the process, they developed pelagic whaling, launching whaleboats directly from their ships. But they still depended on land to render the whales, boiling the blubber in pots on the shores of the Faeroe Islands, Iceland and even the remote coast of Labrador. En route, they hunted both right whales and bowheads – known to Europeans as the Greenland right whale. Recently, a 300-tonne galleon, which sank in 1565, was excavated from the waters of

Red Bay, Labrador, one of the camps maintained by the Basques along the Strait of Belle Isle. The Basques tried out the oil from the blubber of hundreds of bowheads and right whales in Red Bay, and even now, more than 400 years later, the soil around the ruined try-works where blubber was tried out, or rendered, feels greasy.

Although the most profitable, right whales and bowheads were not the only species hunted by Europeans. In 1725 the British naturalist Paul Dudley recorded seeing the only great whale known to have gone extinct since whaling began. The North Atlantic grey whale, with the short baleen of a rorqual and the finless back of a right or bowhead, was hunted as recently as 1640, but it has not been recorded since. The biologists Ole Lindquist and Wim Wolff of the University of Groningen in the Netherlands contend that medieval Europeans hunted this whale until it was extirpated from the eastern Atlantic. Other cetologists remain sceptical that grey whales were ever numerous in the North Atlantic in historic times.

The grey whale did migrate along the east coast of North America, from Canada to Florida, and it is possible that Basque whalers hunted these greys when they expanded their hunt in the sixteenth century. Even if they played no role in the grey whale's demise, the Basques provided the model for whale exploitation that prevailed into the twentieth century. The hunt focused initially on vulnerable females and their slow-swimming, surface-active calves. Whalers then removed young females and males, worth less because they were smaller and more difficult to capture. It was a boom-and-bust industry – once a hunting ground was emptied of whales, the whalers moved on – to new whaling grounds and new species of whales.

The demand for illumination and the rising profits of whaling motivated the English to overcome the formidable barrier of Euskara. In the sixteenth century Queen Elizabeth I awarded

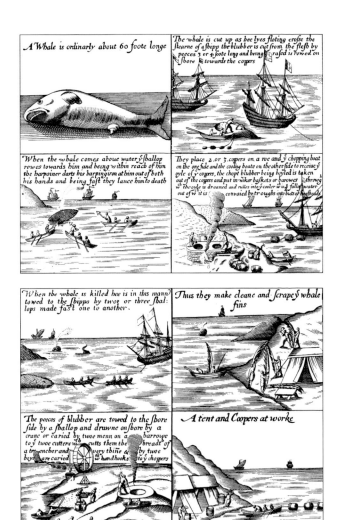

A depiction of whaling in Spitsbergen in 1611, reproduced in *Churchill's Voyages* (1745).

the English Muscovy Company of Merchant Adventurers a monopoly on the right to hunt whales 'within any seas whatsoever'.[14] Basque whalers were hired to man the British ships and teach new crews to whale.[15] In 1607 the English navigator Henry Hudson explored the Arctic for the Muscovy Company. He sailed along the coast of Greenland, discovered the volcanic Jan Mayen Island and reported on the rich whaling grounds 600 kilometres north of Norway in the Arctic Ocean. Soon after Hudson had returned with the news that there were large numbers of bowheads around Spitsbergen, the company sent its first whaling expedition north in 1611. By the end of the decade, the Dutch, Danes and Basques were competing with the English in these whaling grounds.

Before the hunt began, there may have been half a million bowhead whales in the Arctic. Considered 'a heavy loggy fish' with little fight,[16] this large species, which could yield half again as much oil as a full-grown right whale, was especially attractive to whalers willing to risk the ice. Bowhead baleen, with lengths occasionally reaching 4.25 metres (right-whale baleen measures less than 3 m) made the hunt even more profitable.

At first, the whales were tried out on the shores of Spitsbergen, in an area known to the Dutch as the Haarlem Cookery. The head was severed and towed to shore, where the baleen plates were removed, cleaned and tied up in bundles of about 50 plates. The blubber was boiled ashore and shipped back to the Dutch Republic. In these early years, a cartel of about fifteen to twenty ships did all the whaling in the area. The Dutch maritime historian Jaap Bruijn has described this operation as 'an early OPEC'.[17] But the quest for oil soon became a rush, and anybody who could raise the capital sent a vessel north. There was no time to waste ashore; the blubber was packed into casks and sent home. In the Dutch Republic, the try houses were immediately nicknamed stinkeries.[18]

A 1737 engraving of a juvenile bowhead, as most people would have approached it at the time – with a harpoon in its back.

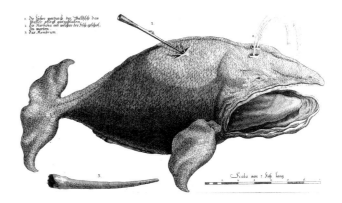

The success of Spitsbergen led to a search for other productive whaling grounds. The Dutch explorer Adriaen Block reported that whales were in great abundance in North America, and the Zwaanendaal colony was established in 1630, in present-day Delaware. Equipped with whaleboats and harpoons, the men were intent on sustaining themselves on proceeds from right whales. No whales were taken, however, and the colony itself became extinct by 1633.[19]

Whalers had to know the migration patterns, the seasonal abundances and the weaknesses and strengths of the whales, just as any predator must know its prey. In 1671 Frederic Marten described bowhead whaling off Spitsbergen:

> To those that are wild we come softly or gently from behind . . . for when the wind is down, the weather calm, and air serene, so that the sea doth not foam or roar, the whales hear immediately the striking of the oars.[20]

They learned to kill the whale as efficiently as possible, for the more time spent in the whaleboat, the longer the cruise and the greater the risk of being iced in. And a whale that was not quickly dispatched could be lost among the pack ice. After the harpoon was set, Martin wrote, the whalers

> launce the whales near their privy-parts . . . for if they are run in there, it doth pain them very much . . . But about the head the harpoon can do him no hurt, because the fat is very *thin* there on the bones, which the whales know as well as we; for when they find themselves in danger, so that they can not escape the harpoon, they rather leave their head than their back undefended, for there the harpoon breaks out easier, and so the whale gets away.[21]

A whale hunt amid icebergs, by the French marine painter Ambroise Louis Garneray, *c.* 1830.

Dutch whaling had its golden age in the 17th and 18th centuries. These Delftware tiles are based on drawings of the Arctic grounds by Sieuwert van der Meulen, *c.* 1720. The target of the hunt, the bow-head, was known as the Greenland right whale, because it was considered a 'loggy fish', with plentiful oil.

When the whale was dead, they cut off the flukes, or tail. Some ships used the flukes and fins as bumpers to protect them from the sharp ice. The whale was secured to the ship, tail forward, head to stern, the blubber was removed and the carcass cut free. Polar bears and seabirds soon descended on the remains.

Whaling was often wasteful – two whales might be killed for every one retrieved and tried out. But the hunt for these ice-loving whales was especially destructive. One observer wrote in 1760: 'they are easily struck and fastened, but not above one third of them are recovered; by sinking and bewildering themselves under the ice, two-thirds of them are lost irrecoverably'.[22]

It was the ice that stirred the greatest fears in the whalers. Ships suffered many a tight squeeze in the great icefields of the north. To get to the bowheads, the British whaler and explorer William Scoresby had his men sally through the fields, with the crew running side to side across the deck to keep the vessel free from ice. But such improvisation could not always beat the Arctic extremes. There was black fog, snowstorms, ice mirages that gave a false horizon and not a single lighthouse. In 1830 nineteen British ships were lost. Few years went by without casualties.

Some crews were picked up by other ships or made it to provisioning stations, where the only food might be rotten meat that had frozen, thawed and frozen again over the years. Even on the ships that remained intact, intolerable conditions reigned, with scurvy on the rise as the winter dragged on. Teeth began to loosen and weakness progressed to the point that men could not leave their bunks. Some died of it; others froze to death in their

Pêche de la baleine by Garnarey is one of the best-known whaling prints. Melville called his 1835 aquatints 'by far the finest . . . presentations of whales and whaling scenes to be found anywhere'.

WONDERS
From the Deep
OR A
True and Exact Account and Defcription
OF THE
Monſtrous Whale,
Lately taken near
COLECHESTER,
Being two and forty Foot in Length, and
of Bigneſs Proportionable.

With the manner of itscoming, and being
Kill'd on *Thurſday* the 9*th*. of *April*.

Being ſo rare and ſtrange a ſight that mul-
titudes of People from all parts dayly go
toſee it as thick as to a Market or Fair.

London Printed for *E. W.* in the Year 1677.

bunks, covered in ice and rime.[23] As one Arctic captain wrote, 'Death and the whalemen touched elbows continuously!'[24]

At its height in the 1680s, the Dutch whale fishery employed about 260 ships and 14,000 sailors. As Spitsbergen stocks declined, both Dutch and British companies whaled along the icy coasts of Greenland. Arctic whalers were killers by occupation, which is not to say that all were cold-hearted. Scoresby remarked on the Arctic hunt for females and calves:

> There is something extremely painful in the destruction of a whale, when thus evincing a degree of affectionate regard for its offspring, that would do honor to the superior intelligence of human beings; yet the object of the adventure, the value of the prize, the joy of the capture, cannot be sacrificed to feelings of compassion.[25]

Hendrick Goltzius created one of the most enduring whale images in his 1598 depiction of a stranded sperm whale.

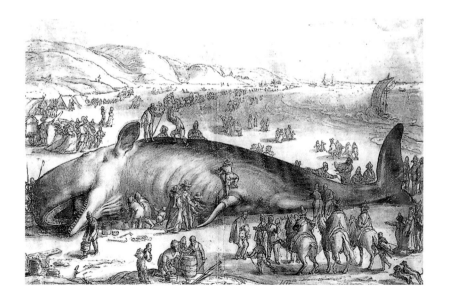

61

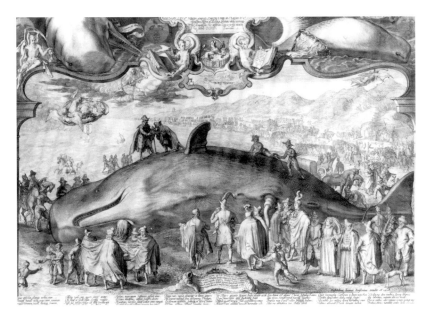

Jan Saenredam's 1602 engraving of a stranded whale near Beverwick emphasized the contemporary belief that such strandings presaged disaster. Father Time's hourglass is running low in the upper left, and is accompanied by melancholy verses.

The typical European, who had never been to sea or aboard a whaleship, had no such conflicts as he lit the oil lamp or she opened her parasol. A few coastal communities would contend with the stinkeries, and gain income from the flow of oil. But, for the most part, there was little opportunity to see a cetacean, whether alive at sea or even stranded on the shore.

Starting in the fifteenth century, illustrated broadsides became an important means of covering events in Europe. Printed in runs of about 1,000 to 2,000 copies, a broadside sold for about half a day's work for the average craftsman. Of the prints devoted to animals, images of whale strandings figured prominently, especially in towns along the coast, from Germany to Spain and around the British Isles. This coverage may have provided the only images of whales that most Europeans would ever see – although whale bones might be on display in a cathedral or travelling show. The broadsides were also an important source of information for sixteenth- and seventeenth-century scientists.

As northern Europeans honed the craft of killing whales, there was a new emphasis, according to Frank, in their depiction of cetaceans, a shift to 'visible features, empirical observation, accurate measurement, and precise recording of data that began to replace the imaginary platonistic rhapsodies of earlier eras'.[26] In other words, artists in the late sixteenth century began to look at the actual 'monsters of the deep' thrust up on shore or chased down by boats, tracing the details of what they saw. One of the most enduring icons was a sperm-whale stranding that occurred in 1598 along the Dutch coast. The Haarlem artist Hendrik Goltzius captured the whale in a remarkably realistic pose (though he had trouble, like many artists before and after, with the fin). The image of this one sperm whale would haunt the natural history books throughout Europe for centuries.

But what did a stranding mean at the time? In the Bering Sea, a drift whale was a gift from Sedna. In Japan, strandings were good luck, the *kujira*, or whale meat, a welcome bounty. But in Europe, where eating whale had fallen out of favour, strandings were thought to be signs of God's anger, a presage of disaster.[27] In a depiction of a stranding near Beverwick in 1601, the iconography that frames the whale augurs an earthquake and a solar and lunar eclipse. Father Time's sand has run out.

A set of sixteen plates based on drawings of the Davis Strait by Sieuwert van der Meulen was etched around 1720 in Amsterdam. To this day, they are considered remarkable for their artistry, historical accuracy and maritime knowledge.[28] Just as the Basque technique of killing whales endured for centuries, these engravings were the provenance of hundreds of images depicting the worldwide quest for whales. Many Europeans, when they thought about whaling at all, conjured up images of polar bears, walruses and the dying bowhead whale, its flipper in the air. An iceberg hung over the scene. It was not until whaling shifted to southern waters and deepwater species that this image changed.

4 Raising Whales

WANTED – Immediately, 100 young men, Americans, to go on
whaling voyages in first class ships. Also Carpenters, Coopers
and Blacksmiths, to whom extra pay will be given. All clothing
and other necessary articles furnished on credit of the voyage.
NB – Voyages from eight months to three years.
New York Tribune, 1 July 1841

There is no life in thee, now, except that rocking life imparted
by a gently rolling ship; by her, borrowed from the sea; by the
sea, from the inscrutable tides of God.
Herman Melville, *Moby-Dick*

God send us whales.
Dean C. Wright, boatsteerer, *Benjamin Rush,* 1841–5

In Europe, the rise of whaling accompanied the shift to an urban
society, which thrived on the artificial light from the whale.
From the start of the European colonization of North America,
whales played a pivotal role in the imperial economy. To
Melville, Yankee whaling was 'that Egyptian mother, who bore
offspring themselves pregnant from her womb'.[1] After the
American Revolution, John Adams implored William Pitt to
open British ports to American whaling products. Without
whale oil, Adams argued, which 'gives the cleanest and most
beautiful flame of any substance known to nature', Britain was in
danger of slipping back to the Dark Ages. 'We are all surprised

that you prefer darkness and consequent robberies, burglaries and murders in your streets to the receiving [of] our spermaceti oil.'[2] The nineteenth-century American statesman Daniel Webster called whaling 'the boldest and most persevering industry'.

Long before books proclaimed the transformative powers of coffee or cod, the pursuit of the whale was considered essential to the rise of modern society. Even present-day cetologists are struck by the influence of their study animals on human culture. As Steven Katona and Hal Whitehead noted, 'The products and capital derived from the whaling industry fuelled the early stages of the industrial revolution that subsequently transformed almost all the world's ecosystems.'[3] We are all riding, if not in the belly of the whale, then on the oil-slick legacy of its blubber.

This was especially true in the waters of eastern North America. The whale was on the minds of many English travellers as they approached North America. Soon after the establishment of the Plymouth Colony, the trade in beaver pelts failed because of over-hunting. The king's commissioners looked to Massachusetts Bay for economic salvation. And, once again, it was the coastal right whale, which migrated from southern nurseries off Florida to northern feeding grounds off Long Island, Cape Cod, the Bay of Fundy, Newfoundland and Labrador, that bore the burden of the hunt.

During the great migration of Puritans in 1635, the English minister Richard Mather rejoiced in the 'multitude of great whales' that became increasingly common as he approached the New World, 'spewing up water in the air like the smoke of a chimney, and making the sea about them white and hoary'.[4] By the time that his grandson Cotton Mather took to the pulpit in Boston, whaling was an important seasonal industry in New England.

To the young Mather, whales were 'Monsters', but they were also worthy of a naturalist's attention, if only to provide worthy metaphors of God's power. Mather lived in two worlds: he believed in witchcraft, working to dismiss the 'spectre' – the visage of an acquaintance seen during a spell – from being used as evidence in witch trials. But he was also an inquisitive scientist, inoculating his own son against smallpox (who almost died from the experiment). As a preacher in whale-rich Massachusetts, Mather used the whale as a parable for God's wrath and magnanimity.

The Whales are a Fish, that sometimes are found of a very Stupendous Magnitude. My Brethren, You that Encounter those mighty Sea-monsters and Extend the Empire of Mankind, unto a Victory and a Dominion over those formidable Animals; most certainly, You ought upon some Accounts to be Christians of the First Magnitude . . . When you have seen what irresistible Blows, the Whale will Strike; and how much the Mighty are afraid, when he raiseth up himself to fetch a Stroke: Don't you hear the Omnipotent GOD, before whom he is no more than a Worm . . . How formidable then will be the Blows of an Almighty GOD upon the objects of his wrath!

A worm before God, perhaps, but the whale could teach way-ward men and women a lesson:

Among the Fish which you follow with your Harping Irons You see the Sea-Monsters draw out the Breast, and give suck to their Young ones: Even in the Cold Sea, such a Warmth of Parental Affection! But what monsters are those Parents, who are Unconcerned, Whether their Children ever Come to Know and Serve God, and Seek and Find the Blessings of the only Savior? Parents, If you never Pray with your Children . . . you are such Monsters. Those of the Sea, do with Open Mouth Cry out against your Cruelty.[5]

Whales may have been monsters, leviathans, even worthy parents, but mostly they were money. In his mercy, God offered the 'Capacious and Voracious Creature' – part right whale, part biblical leviathan – to whalers, so that they could procure their 'Food from the Sale of Him . . . make a Banquet of him, and part him among the Merchants'.[6]

Shore whaling flourished in the seventeenth century. By the 1670s even the schoolmaster's salary was paid in whale oil and baleen in East Hampton, Long Island.[7] The school year ended in December, 'by reson of the Whale Designe', and resumed in April, after the whales had gone and the students were no longer needed to man the boats.[8] Native Americans – the Montauk and the Shinnecock of Long Island – were hired to help in the hunt. Indians had been eating whale meat with peas and maize and roasting 'fynnes and tayles' as sacrifices in religious festivals before Europeans arrived.[9] But historians debate whether they were hunters, with dugout canoes and wooden drogues, or gatherers of drift whales. What is not in doubt is that they comprised crews at

In 1590 Joseph d'Acosta reported that the natives of Florida jumped on the backs of whales and plugged their blowholes with pegs to suffocate them, a no-doubt fanciful technique. Johann Theodor de Bry's engraving of 1602 shows 'the wondrous fishing method of the Indians'.

the outset of colonial whaling. For each whale killed, the natives received cloth coats and half the blubber. The baleen was non-negotiable, belonging exclusively to the colonial entrepreneurs.

Yankee whaling expanded throughout the eighteenth century. By the time of the American Revolution, the colonies were supplying four times the amount of oil to Britain as the entire British fleet in Greenland.[10] Although whaling along the east coast of North America soon declined, new whaling grounds opened up on coastlines around the world: the Dutch started to hunt right whales off South Africa in 1789; the British began hunting humpbacks and right whales in the Pacific and off New Zealand in the 1790s; and through much of the nineteenth century whalers pursued humpbacks, bowheads, right whales and greys from the West Indies to Russia, Madeira and Mexico.[11] Yet from one windswept colonial island, a group of men were about to leave the shore behind.

In the late seventeenth century two mainlanders, James Lopar of Long Island and Ichabod Paddock of Cape Cod, were invited to

Nantucket to teach whaling to the locals, who had been watching the spouts of right whales passing their island for years.[12] The sandy, almost barren island provided little sustenance, and, although the islanders were mostly Quakers, professing a pure doctrine of non-violence, they were quick studies, soon embracing killing of whales. To Melville, these Nantucketers were 'Quakers with a vengeance'. A distant spout, the flash of a glistening black back or the shock of a fluke would prompt the call 'She blows!' from lookouts on shore. The whaleboats were launched into the surf.

Under such vigil, local whales became rare, and the whalers made their way offshore. According to local tradition, Captain Christopher Hussey transformed the whaling industry in 1712. On a voyage to the Nantucket South Shoals, Hussey was blown out to sea, where he sighted numerous single, lopsided blows. In swift pursuit, he and his men killed a spermaceti – the largest odontocete, or toothed whale, with a bulky, fist-shaped head.

Although spermacetis, or sperm whales, lack the valuable baleen of rights, their oil burnt more cleanly and was more stable than baleen-whale oil. Winter strained oil was especially prized; the spermaceti crystallized in the oil in cold temperatures, and the residues and impurities were strained out in the spring and summer. The liquid waxes found in the barrel-shaped spermaceti organ, which makes up most of the sperm whale's enormous head, could be manufactured into candles. A watery fluid at body temperature, spermaceti forms a solid wax when exposed to air. It was the finest candle wax then known, becoming the standard for artificial light. One candlepower is the light from a sperm candle, one sixth of a pound, burning at two grains per hour.

Nantucket soon had one of the largest whaling ports in North America. The words *Nantucketer* and *whaleman* became synonymous, and the tethered race of a whaleboat behind a harpooned whale was called a Nantucket sleigh ride. The pursuit of the sperm whale changed whaling from a shore-based chase to a pelagic, or oceanic, hunt – a voyage. Nantucket whalers developed a new method for trying out the whale. In the traditional European method, whalers cut the blubber of the whale at sea and stored it in casks to be refined at home. In the 1760s Nantucketers began to build ovens on their vessels – a 3 by 2.5 metre erection of brickwork – and the whale was tried out in great iron pots on deck. This innovation was probably devised to accommodate the warm-water preferences of sperm whales; although fine in the Arctic, casks of blubber spoilt quickly in the tropical waters preferred by sperm whales.

As a result of this shift, communities were no longer directly involved in the hunt for whales. The shore-based lookouts began to disappear, as did the onshore try-works. Men raised whales at sea. The blubber was removed, or flensed, on the open ocean, and the whale was reduced to its products – sperm oil, whale oil, baleen – before it reached the shore. In ports, a whale was a cask of oil, covered in seaweed to protect it from the sun on the dock, or a bundle of bone. To a city dweller, the whale was reduced to the light from a lamp or the hourglass figure of a corset stay.

After the American Revolution, sperm oil illuminated the city streets of the new nation, and spermaceti candles were in great demand. Tallow candles from the Old World disappeared.[13] New England fleets expanded rapidly. Nantucket threw itself into whaling: onshore were the coopers, riggers, sailmakers, boat-builders, blacksmiths, millers and farmers; at sea, the forecastle hands, shipmasters, steersmen and ship-keepers. Ashore, the men wore long dark coats and wide-brimmed hats. The boatsteerers, the hunters who harpooned the whales, wore chock pins from the bow of the whaleboat in their lapels. Often made of oak, though some were fashioned from the bone of the whale itself, these pins advertised the bachelor's status as he gambolled around town – for there were rumours that some young women would only marry a man who had killed a whale.[14]

According to Herman Melville, the quest for oil and bone resulted in open battle. Nantucket whalers 'in all seasons and all oceans declared everlasting war with the mightiest animated mass that has survived the flood; most monstrous and most mountainous!'[15] Given this war at sea, is it any wonder that Emanuel Leutze perched the Revolutionary general on a whale-boat when he composed *Washington Crossing the Delaware* in 1851? And was the man on the bow harpooning a block of ice as they crossed to New Jersey? No high-walled barge, the common transport for troops in the eighteenth century, would do for George Washington. He joined the eminent whaling families, the Coffins and the Morgans, as a man of the blubber. Or per-haps it was just that Leutze found the common whaleboat to be the closest prop at hand.

Nantucket life was whaling. The French-born writer and Nantucket farmer J. Hector St John de Crévecoeur described the education of the island's children:

At school they learn to read, and to write a good hand, until they are twelve years old; they are then in general put apprentices to the cooper's trade, which is the second essential branch of business followed here; at fourteen, they are sent to sea, where in their leisure hours their com-panions teach them the art of navigation, which they have an opportunity of practicing on the spot. They learn the great and useful art of working a ship in all the different situations which the sea and wind so often require . . . Then they go gradually through every station of rowers, steersmen, and harpooners; thus they learn to attack, to pursue, to overtake, to cut, to dress their huge game: and after having performed several such voyages . . . they are fit either for the counting-house or chase.[16]

Nantucketer Obed Macy wrote that to the mariner, the sea is just a highway, 'but to the whaler it is his field of labor'.[17] Many of these labourers were greenhands, new to the field. Although whale oil was valuable, greenhands received only meagre rations and earnt no wages. They were paid a fraction of the profits, often less than $1/200$ of the net proceeds. Even on successful voyages, this hardly covered the clothes and tobacco many purchased from the ship's stores. On a poor voyage, a new whale-man could return to New Bedford, after several years at sea, owing money to the owners.

So what drew them to whaling? Some might have been lured by what Baudelaire called the 'profound and mysterious charm that arises from looking at a ship'; others, as Elizabeth Hardwick noted in her biography of Melville, 'have come sulking away, address unknown, from howling creditors, accusing wives, alert policemen, beggary on shore'.[18] Many greenhands were from farming families, some awaiting their inheritance, others, as younger sons, unlikely to come into anything. Runaway slaves were not uncommon aboard Yankee whalers: Nantucket's Quaker population helped to secure berths for those in danger of being recaptured by bounty hunters.

A few months in the forecastle, a hole at the bow of the ship just forward of the blubber room, was enough to disabuse many green-hands of any romantic notions about life at sea. As many as 21 men bunked in this 3-by-5-metre room, which could be overcast with 'a thick dark cloud of tobacco smoke', occasionally cut by the growls of the foremast hands. 'How I detest this fore castle', 19-year-old

'She blows!' The long-awaited call from the masthead. An illustration from J. Ross Browne's *Etchings of a Whaling Cruise* (1846).

Enoch Cloud wrote one Sunday, 'in which lewd songs for those of Zion & blasphemous wraths, for notes of prayer & praise are exchanged!'[19]

A typical vessel was 300 tons, not much more than 30 metres from bow to square stern, with two decks and three square-rigged masts. The decks were constructed of white pine, but the rest of the ship – from the ribs to the planking – was oak.[20] It was broad in the beam to accommodate the brick try-works, iron cauldrons, davits for the boats and the space to try out the whale.[21] To someone accustomed to a clipper, the flat-bottomed whale-ship could feel as if it wobbled 'all around like a drunken tailor with two left legs'.[22] A large ship might be equipped with four boats, three on the port and one on the starboard side, where the cutting-in was done after a whale was captured.[23] Upon sighting a whale, the lookout shouted 'Blows!' or 'She blows!', and the boats would be lowered to begin the chase. A whaleboat was about 8 metres long, sharp at both ends in case it was turned around in the chase, and held five oarsmen and a harpooner. An American whaling ship might hold 25 to 35 men. According to Ellis:

> The captain might earn $1/8$ of $1/10$ of the net proceeds, while a mate could earn $1/15$ and a harpooner $1/90$. Ordinary seamen could hope at best for $1/150$, and there are instances in the records where a greenhand signed aboard for $1/350$. What did this mean in terms of actual money? . . . During the six consecutive voyages totaling 1,218 days at sea from 1845 to 1868, the average lay per voyage on the Salem whaler *James Maury* was $321.21, or about 26 cents a day. This compared unfavorably to wages then being paid to unskilled workers . . . but landlubbers did not get to visit exotic Pacific Islands where they might be eaten by cannibals, or risk their lives fighting gigantic whales.[24]

Ishmael claimed that his voyage aboard the *Pequod* was 'my Yale College and my Harvard', but not everyone saw a voyage as an education. The boatsteerer, Dean Wright, wrote of the green-hands: 'they have got to spend three or four years in the prime of their life in a business which they do not understand, and from which they will not recover any thing commensurate to the time spent'.[25] Although there were probably a few at university who would tell you that Ishmael's claim and the boatsteerer's lament were not mutually exclusive, for those who stuck with whaling, a decent living could be made as an officer.

The rhythm of life aboard ship survives in the chanteys sung when hoisting sail or cutting-in whales. Whalers who had fished the South Pacific might be familiar with 'A Long Time Ago' ...

I made up my mind to go to sea
I made up my mind to go to sea

I wish to God I'd never been born
To go rambling round and round Cape Horn

Around Cape Horn where wild winds blow
Around Cape Horn with sleet and snow ...
Around Cape Horn with frozen sails,
Around Cape Horn to fish for whales.[26]

By the time they reached the Horn, many young men may have promised themselves never to go whaling again. And whalers were young. It was not unusual to find twelve-year-olds in the forecastle. At seventeen, a determined teenager could find himself on the bow of a whaleboat, darting his first whale.

The greenhands, by necessity, were taught the ropes at sea. The captain distributed them among the boats, so as not to slow its progress when they inevitably caught a crab with their oars, breaking the rhythm of the boat. From the stern, the mate called out 'Break your backs!' as each took an oar. It was best to be quick, for the 'iron-fisted and iron-hearted officers' often 'beat their information in with anything that came to hand'.[27]

Approaching the first sperm whale, perhaps twice the size of the boat with an enormous fist-shaped head, must have been one of the most exhausting and terrifying moments of a green-hand's young life. Evolutionary biologists suggest that the bull whale's size and the great mass of head in front of his eyes developed as a battering ram to injure rival whales. During the attack, males also rake their teeth along their opponent's head.

On occasion, the whales used these weapons to attack their terrestrial assailants. Captain Wood of the *Emeline* was killed by a whale in July 1842; the brig returned to New Bedford the following year with only ten barrels of oil after a 26-month cruise. In 1851 a whale attacked a whaleboat, 'crushing it into fragments as small as a common-sized chair'.[28] It went on to attack a second boat, and then struck the ship, 'knocking a great hole entirely through her bottom'.[29] The crew was picked up the following day.

The most famous attack was on the whale-ship *Essex* in 1819. 'In one short moment', wrote the first mate, Owen Chase, 'the

This sketch by a harpooner aboard the *Charles W. Morgan* shows the bigger-than-life impression that the sperm whale's size made on the whalers.

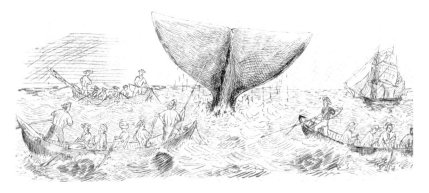

76

crew had been cut off from all the hopes and prospects of the living.' A bull whale attacked the ship, capsizing it, and swam off with no apparent injury, although remaining in sight for several hours. The crew tied their boats together on the lee side of the ship. That night, the whale invaded Chase's dreams: 'the dismal looking wreck, and the horrid aspect and revenge of the whale, wholly engrossed my reflections, until day again made its appearance.' He was convinced that the whale had attacked the ship deliberately.[30]

Although they were close to Tahiti, the captain and crew decided to strike out for South America, more than 3,000 kilometres to the east. On their decision to avoid the Society Islands, the captain noted: 'we feared we should be devoured by cannibals if we cast ourselves on their mercy'.[31]

The men of the *Essex* were left with meagre rations: at first half a biscuit and a pint of water a day. After ten days, they ate the Galápagos tortoise rescued from the ship's stores. The rations were halved and then halved again as the days beneath 'the hot rays of the sun . . . bore upon our health and spirits with an amazing force and severity'.[32] After two months at sea, the weakened castaways found themselves surrounded by whales; they took fright at 'the terrible noise of whale-spouts'. Listening to the spouts and thrashing of the tails, Chase noted, 'our weak minds pictured out their appalling and hideous aspects'. The men were too weak to 'raise a single arm in [their] own defence'; 'blowing and spouting at and a terrible rate', the whales passed the stern of the boat and disappeared.[33]

After two and a half months, there was nothing left but the skin and bones of the crew. On Chase's boat, the body of Isaac Cole, instead of being disposed of at sea, was prepared for food. The crew devoured his heart, then dried and roasted the flesh to serve them for the following days. On the captain's boat, faced with starvation after the consumption of the dead, four men cast lots. Owen Coffin was shot and eaten.

The five men who survived went on to command ships. Chase filled the *Charles Carrol* twice with 2,600 barrels of sperm oil. In his final years, it was said, he took to hiding food in the attic of his Nantucket home.[34] The whaling community now had its legends.

The best whalers were highly valued and so spent most of their lives at sea. J. N. Reynolds wrote on meeting an especially prized first mate:

> so intimately did he seem acquainted with the habits and instincts of the objects of his pursuit, and so little conversant with the ordinary affairs of life; that one felt less inclined to class him in the genus *homo*, than as a sort of intermediate something between man and the cetaceous tribe.[35]

A good harpooner was invaluable, although Wright griped that his position was, of all the berths of a whale-ship, 'the most disagreeable and thankless . . . A man who has been one voyage in the whaling business and then will ship again to do a boat-steerer's duty must be either mad or drunk, or else a fool or a saint.'[36]

Coming on to the whale, after perhaps a mile of rowing, the boatsteerer was ordered to stand and face the quarry. He would grab the top harpoon, the newest and sharpest, on the starboard bow and brace his left thigh against the clumsy cleat, a notch in the prow. 'Give it to him!' the mate would cry, and the boatsteerer heaved the iron. The line was paid out and snubbed at the loggerhead, doused with water to keep it from bursting into flame.

The boat might race across the surface, tugged behind the whale as it tried to escape its fate. If the whale didn't sound too deep, forcing the mate to cut the line, this fate was in his hands – in the form of a 3.5-metre lance, or killing iron, with a leaf-shaped blade to pierce the whale's vital organs.

'Chimney's afire!' the mate would call, when the lance found its mark, usually the lungs or heart, and the blow became a burning bush of blood. Once the fatal lance was given, 'the blood from the nostril' was 'frequently thrown upon the men in the boats, who glory in its show!' Just before the whale's death, the British surgeon Thomas Beale observed, 'the whole strength of its enormous frame is set in motion for a few seconds, when his convulsions throw him into a hundred different contortions of the most violent description, by which the sea is beaten into a foam, and boats are sometimes crushed to atoms, with their crews'.[37] The first mate and raconteur Frank Bullen noted that

W. J. Huggins's aquatint of 1834 of boats attacking a sperm whale was one of the greatest whaling images of the 19th century, providing a prototype for many subsequent depictions of the South Sea hunt.

this last flurry was followed by silence. 'A short spell of gradually-quieting struggle succeeded as the great beast succumbed, until all was still again, except the strange, low surge made by the waves as they broke over the bank of flesh passively obstructing their free sweep.'[38]

The response, according to the American sperm-whaling song 'There She Blows', was jubilance:

> A lance in her life and the struggle is finished
> So slowly she sinks with her chimney on fire
> Loud rings the joyful sound from each stout seaman's heart
> Matching the sea in its turbulent roar
> Look from the spout hole see the red signals fly
> So slowly she dies and the struggle is o'er.[39]

Despite the 'joyful' sounds, some on the boats had mixed emotions. After his ship had struck a right whale, Enoch Cloud wrote:

> she quickly 'slued' around, raised her enormous head out of the water, fixed her eyes on the boat, and then bellowing commenced, slowly, 'sterning off.'
>
> It was the most terrible sight I ever witnessed . . . It is painful to witness the death of the smallest of God's created beings, much more one in which life is so vigorously maintained as the Whale! And when I saw this, the largest and most terrible of all created animals bleeding, quivering, dying a victim to the cunning of man, my feelings were indeed peculiar![40]

Whalers may not have expressed much sympathy with their quarry, but the death of a mother with calf could break even the toughest façade: 'That's when you feel it', said one whaler, 'when we killed the mother the milk made the ocean white all around us.'[41]

After the long chase and the laborious haul back to the ship, the real work began. A foremast hand was often in charge of revving the heavy chains through the massive jaw and around the flukes, fastening the whale to the ship head to stern. A dead whale in heavy seas was almost as dangerous as a living one. As the writer Robert McNally later described it, 'Swinging gear and blubber pieces, knives and spades, a pitching deck, and hordes of sharks attracted to the carcass could maim or kill and often did.'[42]

Whaling, of course, was not a rehearsed ballet, but a struggle that varied from ship to ship, whale to whale, and day to day. Even when whales were fast to the ship, they could be lost in gales, since cutting-in was all but impossible in foul weather. Heads could be ripped from their chains, with the loss of hundreds of pounds of spermaceti. Or worse, as storms raged, the whale expanded, rising above the deck like a mountain in the swell.

Suddenly, with a roar like the bursting of a dam, the pent up gases tore their furious way out of the distended carcass, hurling the entrails in one horrible entanglement widespread over the sea . . . the unutterable fœtor wrought its poisonous way back through that fierce, pure blast, permeating every nook of the ship with its filthy vapour till the stoutest stomach there protested in unmistakable terms against such vile treatment . . . the skipper gave orders to cut the corrupt mass adrift. Away went eight hundred pounds worth of oil.[43]

If the seas allowed it, the cutting stages were lowered from a series of tackles, and the whale was rotated in the water, its blubber, according to Melville, 'stripped off from the body precisely as an orange is sometimes stripped by spiralizing it'.[44] The head was removed and the blubber cut into blankets about 4.5 metres long, weighing a tonne. On a well-run ship, blankets rose in quick succession. They were typically lowered into the main hatch or blubber room, where they were cut into smaller pieces, and these were sliced into books or bibles on long planks on the deck, the blubber spreading out from the skin like the splayed pages of a ponderous tome. The bible leaves were placed in the try-pots and boiled to remove the oil. Tried out, the fritters, or the unmelted skin of the whale, were skimmed off the top and used to feed the flames. As the whale was processed, the cooper assembled the casks, which had been stored as a bundle of used staves, or shooks, to save space. A typical whale took about 36 hours to process.

At the end of the day, a whale was just a stamp in a logbook, the number of barrels inscribed in its flank. The average female yielded about 30 to 35 barrels of oil, the largest bulls up to 90,[45] about 11,000 litres or enough to fill a small swimming pool. The oil from a typical whale would light a signal lamp for almost a decade or keep a lighthouse beaming for up to a year. With the oil burnt off long ago, all that remains of most of the whales that were killed are the monotonous logs: *Janis* 1843: 'Whale . . . do . . . do . . . do . . . Left Desolation Island for the North'. *Robert Edwards* 1864: 'got one . . . got one . . . got one . . .'.

Whalers, almost to a man, were more concerned with daily sustenance and the number of barrels aboard than they were with the whales themselves. Once they had their sea legs, the green-

Charles Scammon's outline of the method of cutting-in a sperm whale in the 19th century.

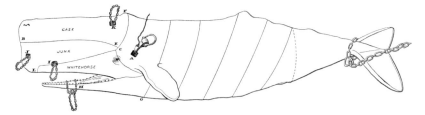

hands would venture to try the 'grub'. ('I cannot libel "food"', wrote Bullen, 'by using it in such a connection'.) For supper: 'A bit of salt junk and a piece of bread, i.e. biscuit, flinty as a pantile, with a pot of something sweetened with "longlick" (molasses) made an apology for a meal.'[46] Given such meagre rations, porpoises caught at sea were especially welcome. Not only did they supply some oil, helping to shorten the trip, but porpoise beef, when decently cooked, was also excellent eating for 'the poor half-starved wretches' of the whaler's crew. The tight rations caused resentment between the forecastle and the captain's quarters. Cloud wrote in his journal in 1852:

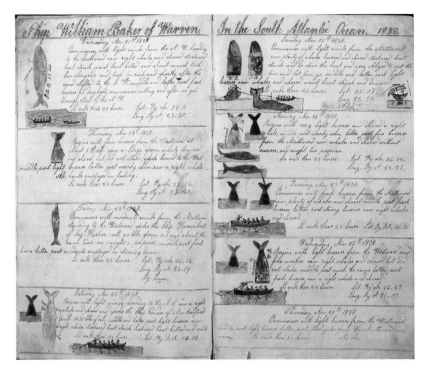

After the oil had burnt, logbooks were often all that remained of the whales that were hunted in the 19th century.

Work is nothing – but we do not get enough to eat! Capt. Vinall's soul (which would occupy but a small space in a mosquito's bladder) is gifted with a very large stock of – selfishness! He satisfies his own palate, with the best, while the crew can not get enough – hard-bread & salt meat! Will come Whaling-eh?!!!![47]

It is no surprise that a stop at the Galápagos Islands was treated with great relish. All hands were employed in the hunt for tortoises. Because they could be stowed for months, Galápagos tortoises were highly treasured by whalers, desperate for fresh meat, and by a captain hoping to extend an unlucky voyage and reverse his fortune. Although the turtles were thought to have a 'disagreeable appearance, very much resembling a large serpent', their flesh was considered 'very good'.[48] The slow-moving reptiles were easy prey; in five days in 1848, the *Daniel Lincoln* took 273 tortoises from Chatam Island alone. With tens of thousands of tortoises removed by whalers, many islands were soon emptied of adults. Introduced rats removed the remaining eggs. Whaling certainly altered ocean ecosystems by removing large predators, but it also caused extinctions on the Pacific islands themselves.

At South Sea ports, such as Samoa, whalers replenished their galleys 'with yams, poultry, pigs, coconuts, tropical fruit, water, and firewood'.[49] As hogs boarded, disgruntled men deserted. Locals were often recruited or kidnapped to fill the empty berths. Many of those who stayed on vowed never to whale again. One young man wrote to his mother from the *Junior* in 1860: 'whales are very scarce this season . . . and every one is

The relative proportions of the baleen of the whalebone whales:
1 bowhead
2 right
3 fin
4 humpback
5–7 grey whale

down hearted and have given up all hopes of a voyage . . . The man that gets me whaleing again after I get home will have to give me the Ship to do it.'[50]

Even captains suffered from long years away from home. Charles Weeks wrote to his wife from the South Atlantic:

> March 20, 1830
> I should rather go with t[w]o meals per day & be with my dear wife than have all the luxuries that this wourld can afford & be separated $9/10$ of the time I here by the Bearer of this letter that Hiram had 1500 bbls last November and the Iris 1200.
>
> November 24, 1830
> I am determined that the ocean shall never separate us again not as long as we can live in love and harmony with each other and no grate loss of property befalls us perhaps you will say that I roat you so before . . . I never was so sick of the sea as I now am and not only the sea but the separation from my dear wife. There she blows so I must q[u]it riting.[51]

Despite his conflict between devotion and oil, Weeks may have been true to his word, for there is no record of his having commanded a ship again. Most captains, however, having worked their way from the forecastle to the stern, spent the majority of their adult lives at sea. They may have looked forward to the voyage that would enable them to retire, but for many this day would never come. Captain Nathanial Skiff Smith's obituary in the *Vineyard Gazette* described a typical captain's life: 'He had been an exile from home for nearly 35 years, having spent about 5 years of this time with his family.' Captain Smith died shortly after his last voyage.[52]

Given the time away from home and the relatively spacious quarters on board, some captains took their families on voyages.

They had to reimburse the owners for this privilege, which could cost as much as $1,000 for a wife alone. A daughter born in the Azores, en route to whaling grounds in the Pacific, recalled: 'As soon as a whale was brought alongside, my mother began preparations to get ready for the dirty time there would be on ship. I was dressed in a dark brown calico (it always seemed to me it need not have been quite so homely) and an old pair of shoes.' After a few years at sea, the entire family's wardrobe would be permeated with the stink of boiling whale oil. Perhaps just as bad from the point of view of the captain's wife, her clothes would surely have gone out of fashion since her departure.[53]

By the mid-nineteenth century, New Bedford, Massachusetts, had replaced Nantucket as the centre of Yankee whaling. In 1850 the *Amethyst* of New Bedford departed for the Pacific Ocean, returning with 2,300 barrels of sperm oil after 45 months at sea. The *Liverpool*, also of New Bedford, gathered more than 22,000 lb of whalebone and almost 2,000 barrels of whale oil. The *Ann Alexander* of New Bedford was sunk by a whale after sending 115 barrels of sperm oil home. *America, 2d*, was crushed by ice in the Anadir Sea. *Jane Howes* of Provincetown, Massachusetts, sailed the North Atlantic for five months and returned with only 160 barrels of sperm oil. Captain Browne of the *Odd Fell*ow departed from Sag Harbor, Long Island. He was later killed while cutting-in a whale. These were just a few of the 203 voyages that departed that year as recorded by Alexander Starbuck in his comprehensive *History of the American Whale Fishery from its Very Inception to the Year 1876*.[54]

The year 1850: Edgar Allen Poe and John James Audubon have just died in New York City – Poe in abject poverty and Audubon in the midst of his *Viviparous Quadrupeds of North America*. Lieutenant M. F. Maury is at work on a map of whale distributions throughout the oceans of the world, a classic still consulted by historians and biologists today. Charles M. Scammon is sailing to California from his native Maine; soon disenchanted with digging for gold, he would find a whaling brig to command and later write one of the nineteenth century's finest zoological studies of marine mammals. Thoreau is revising *Walden*. A journalist in Brooklyn, Walt Whitman, is writing poems that will appear in a slim volume called *Leaves of Grass*. Harriet Beecher Stowe, an ardent abolitionist, is writing *Uncle Tom's Cabin; or, Life Among the Lowly*; when it is published the following year, *Uncle Tom's Cabin* helps to solidify Northern opposition to slavery, leading to the American Civil War. Nineteen-year-old Emily Dickinson begins composing verse in Amherst, Massachusetts, writing to a former schoolmate: 'The shore is safer, Abiah, but I love to buffet the sea – I count the bitter wrecks here in these pleasant waters, and hear the murmuring winds, but oh, I love the danger!'[55] Herman Melville, the celebrated author of *Typee*, a novel based on travels aboard a whaler in the South Pacific, is whipping up his latest whaling yarn, overdue at his London publishers. After meeting Nathaniel Hawthorne in the Berkshire Mountains, he moves to Arrowhead, a 160-acre farm near Hawthorne's home. Melville spends all of 1850 and most of 1851 transforming his adventure into *Moby-Dick*.

For we must address it, that 'gorgeous phantasmagoria',[56] the 900-pound, no, the 50-ton leviathan in the room: *Moby-Dick*. Born in New York in 1819, Melville had worked as a clerk, served on the crew of a merchant ship, and taught at a school in Greenbush, New York, until he was let go because the board could not pay his salary. On 3 January 1841 he sailed on the whaler *Acushnet* from Fairhaven, Massachusetts, bound for the Pacific. Melville's voyage lasted about eighteen months before he deserted. The journey would alter the course of American literature.

Ahab confronts
Moby Dick in the
frontispiece of the
1899 edition of
Melville's novel.

In *Moby-Dick*, Melville relied on his own experiences aboard the *Acushnet*, but the book was also an opportunity to take on an *entire* literature. He had 'swum through libraries' to capture his quarry, plotting his course by the whaling literature (including William Scoresby, Thomas Beale, Francis Allyn Olmsted, F. D. Bennett and J. Ross Browne), his own experience and the 'puns and innuendoes' that gust though the novel.[57] As early as May 1850, Melville was aware of the new tack his 'whaling voyage' was taking. He wrote to the maritime writer Richard Henry Dana:

> It will be a strange sort of book, tho', I fear; blubber is blubber you know; tho' you may get oil out of it, the poetry runs as hard as sap from a frozen maple tree; – & to cook the thing up, one must needs throw in a little fancy, which from the nature of the thing, must be ungainly as the gambols of the whales themselves. Yet I mean to give the truth of the thing, spite of this.[58]

Although 'this strange sort of book' was received with mixed reviews, most critics agreed that Melville had given truth to one thing: the whales themselves. According to the *Atlas* magazine in London, *Moby-Dick* contained

> a mass of knowledge touching the whale – its habitats and its history – the minutest details of its feeding and sporting, or swimming, strangely mixed with ingenious and daring speculations on the mysterious habits and peculiarities of the great brute – the whole written in a tone of exaltation and poetic sentiment which has a strange effect upon the reader's mind.[59]

Even today, scientific articles refer to Melville's minutest details and daring speculations when addressing the biology and behaviour of the sperm whale.

It was more than just the greatest American novel. Readers saw the white whale everywhere. The whale was fate;[60] 'the cosmic will incarnate';[61] Satan, the 'great demon of the sea'; and even God. [62] By rendering humans puny and insignificant, the whale was sublime, a natural force that could not and should not be subdued.[63] All that, and a tome with the pleasurable heft of a bible, or a sperm-whale tooth.

The early reviewers were divided. The *Southern Quarterly Review* for example, called the book 'Sad stuff, dull and dreary, or ridiculous'. *Bentley's Miscellany* noted that it was 'one of the most remarkable of books which has appeared for many years past'.[64] A commercial failure, few nineteenth-century readers knew about this whale at all. *Moby-Dick* sounded from the public consciousness. Long out of print, it resurfaced around the centenary of Melville's birth in 1919 as an American classic. Since then, dissertations, literary criticism, biographies, sea vocabularies, even a picture gallery of all the prints mentioned in the novel, have tried-out *Moby-Dick* for libraries around the world.

Is there any animal with greater name recognition? I turned to www.googlefight.com. Moby Dick appeared on 588,000 websites, beating Bugs Bunny (530,000), but losing to Mickey Mouse (1,250,000) and King Kong (1,110,000). He easily beat his old rival Ahab (193,000) along with his creator (Herman Melville had 230,000). The entire text is now available online for free. Term papers are extra.

Since 1996 devotees of the white whale, including Congressmen, schoolteachers, retired pastors and whaling historians, have gathered in New Bedford every year to commemorate the embarkation of the *Acushnet*. They read Melville's deathless prose in English, of course, but also in

Japanese, Portuguese, Italian and Iñupiaq. The murky smell of whale, a sweet combination of oil and brine, is thick in the room. Occasionally a drop of oil leaches onto the slate floor.

Among the many dichotomies in the book, Starbuck, the first mate, and Flask, the third, have entirely different approaches to their prey. 'I will have no man in my boat', Starbuck says, 'who is not afraid of a whale.'[65] He fears and venerates the whale, whereas Flask tolerates no such awe. Melville, who wrote the best descriptions of early nineteenth-century whaling, also foretold the era of factory whaling:

> So utterly lost was Flask to all sense of reverence for the many marvels of their majestic bulk and mystic ways; and so dead to anything like an apprehension of any possible danger from encountering them; that in his poor opinion, the wondrous whale was but a species of magnified mouse, or at least water-rat, requiring only a little circumvention and some small application of time and trouble in order to kill and boil.[66]

Kill and boil; produce and consume. The Italian writer Roberto Calasso noted in *The Ruin of Kasch*:

> Melville raises literature to butchery, pushes it beyond an unheard-of threshold, imposes on the page what we always knew was happening, but happening offstage and outside the word. 'The ivory Pequod was turned into a shambles; every sailor a butcher.' Literature had blossomed out of sacrifice, but it had never before described the act of butchery; rather it had been the labyrinthine garland around the void. With Melville, butchery becomes the actual center of the book.[67]

Indeed, butchery has been at the centre of the relationship between men and whales since the rise of commercial whaling. Ishmael, however, prefers the metaphor of war: 'what disordered slippery decks of a whale-ship are comparable to the unspeakable carrion of those battle-fields from which so many soldiers return to drink in all ladies' plaudits?'[68]

To the whales, it must have seemed a massacre. A whaleman may have been bored, lonely, cold or uncomfortable, or suffered the blows of a frustrated captain, but the hunt was a terrifying chase for the whale, often ending in the agony of a harpoon, made worse by the drag of a whaleboat and stab of the lance at every attempt to breathe. For those struck whales that escaped by sounding, death may have come more slowly after the whalers cut the line, by a spreading infection or sharks and killer whales attracted to the wound. Such hidden mortality may have taken hundreds of thousands of whales over the course of whaling history.

The blame for these lost whales would sometimes turn to the impure actions and thoughts of the crew, an unexpected echo of the cleansing rituals of the Arctic whalers. Mary Colson, aboard the barque *George and Susan* with her husband Captain Herbert Colson, wrote in her journal in November 1877:

Today is the fifteenth day we have seen whales. Sperm whales four times. Got only two so far. It is kinder hard on us but it is for the best I suppose. Herbert thinks some of us must be awful wicked to deserve such punishment. Chased right whales this morning, then sperm and right again tonight. Got none isn't it awful.[69]

Perhaps to fend off such wickedness, bibles were sometimes distributed at the start of voyages, and some captains read to their crew on Sundays. But few Sunday ships, as the pious vessels were known, held strictly to the Sabbath. Although religious observances were required and swearing was banned on the deck of some whalers, Sunday became, as Frank notes, 'just another workday – perhaps with a meal of plum duff thrown in for formality's sake'.[70]

Sperm and right whales were the preferred prey of Yankee whalers. Yet a whole school of sperm whales could disappear 'as if by magic in the dazzling path of the late sun'.[71] An unsuccessful cruise might prompt an attack on any passing cetacean, perhaps out of frustration or boredom. Enoch Cloud:

> 10 AM A 'finback' came up and 'blowed' immediately alongside. He continued to swim around the ship for some time 'til at length, Capt. Vinall became vexed at his familiarity, mounted the rail and gave him a lance! It penetrated through his blubber, not hurting him much but enough to 'remind him of an engagement downtown!' He left for parts unknown![72]

A passing ship was a welcome break in the monotony – a chance to socialize, or gam. On Nantucket, a gam was a group of whales; at sea, the gam became a group of whale-ships, gathered to gossip and exchange news. Melville was given the published account of the sinking of the whale-ship *Essex*, during a gam. Perhaps lasting several hours, sometimes days, boats were often in constant motion between the ships. The foremast hands could swap presents, fruit perhaps or wine, and complain – to someone new. In the evening, as John Martin wrote aboard the *Lucy Ann*, there might be 'singing music and deviltry'.[73]

More often than not, however, a passing ship was just a holler – 'How many barrels?' – with the oil and time recorded in the logs: 'Spoke ship *Euphrates* of New Bedford 25 months out 2700.

Bound direct home. Sent letters by her'. 'Spoke ship *Almira* 8 months out 350 bbls'. '25 months out 1700 bbls. sperm'.

Boredom was one of the biggest threats on board. The boat-steerer Dean Wright noted in his journal:

> I do not know what to write and I only undertake it because I *can't* do anything else . . . And for the last three or four months I have looked for whales hard – pulled hard on the boats, worked hard on board – and have done next to nothing – which is *very hard*.[74]

From the tedium of these oil-soaked decks, an indigenous art form arose. Around 1825 whalers began to carve and engrave images on the discarded bones and teeth of their quarry – a practice they called scrimshaw. Before this time, sperm-whale teeth had been highly valuable in Polynesia – a closely guarded secret among the sailors who visited Pacific ports of call. During the War of 1812 the American commodore David Porter took his squadron around Cape Horn to attack British whalers. His published account emphasized the value of sperm-whale teeth – and the market soon crashed. Classic whaler's scrimshaw rose from the surplus. The scrimshander's canvas was the tear-shaped tooth of the sperm whale, with its reassuring heft, a walrus tusk, a whale jawbone or baleen. The jackknife, that 'omnipotent tool of the sailor', according to Melville, was his brush.[75]

In this new nineteenth-century art form, there were no rules and few precedents. Although whales were the medium, they were rarely the message. Scrimshaw depicted home life, patriotic portraits, family scenes, naval engagements, the women back home, or, most famously, those encountered at sea. Some took as their subjects the details of life that surrounded them: ships,

The 'Spectre Whalemen', a whaleboat and crew lost in the fogs of the South Pacific, was one of many legends that sprang from the fears of 19th-century whalers.

rigging and knots, figureheads and anchors, even the constellations Cetus and Delphis. Only occasionally did a scrimshander carve a whaling scene, and it was decidedly the whaling, not the whale, that took centre bone. Like chanteys, these motifs were often copies or variations of the work of other men on board.

Whalers engraved teeth and pan bone for relatives and friends; elaborate swifts for winding yarn, jagging wheels for edging pies, glove stretchers, even boot jacks for their wives; and logbook stamps, tattoo needles, tooth extractors, persuaders (large bone clubs for taking seals and walruses), and back-scratchers (more than just a luxury, given the quantity of vermin aboard) for themselves and their shipmates.[76]

These carvings are what remain of the endless time waiting for whales at sea, time that would drag on as whale populations declined and voyages lengthened, and they are almost all that is left of the whales themselves, who lit the night, oiled the first wheels of the Industrial Revolution and vanished into the depths.

Feel the soil in Red Bay, Labrador, still oily from the onshore try-works. Listen to Portuguese on the piers of Massachusetts, echoes of the ships that took many Azoreans to the United States. Enter the New Bedford Whaling Museum and you're overwhelmed by the sweet unctuous scent of whale. Step onto the cobbled streets of this great whaling port, where, Ralph Waldo Emerson remarked, 'they hug an oil-cask like a brother'.[77] Mansions once lined these streets; several remain on New London's Whale Oil Row. 'Whence came they?' Melville wondered.

> Go and gaze upon the iron emblematical harpoons round yonder lofty mansion, and your question will be answered. Yes; all these brave houses and flower gardens came from the Atlantic, Pacific, and Indian Oceans. One and all they were harpooned and dragged up hither from the bottom of the sea.[78]

Dragged up, like the whale-bone houses on the Arctic shore. Stroll among the descendants of the harpoon. In New Bedford, Melville wrote: 'fathers, they say, give whales for dowers to the daughters and portion off their nieces with a few porpoises a-piece'.[79] Walk along the shore, where nearly every cottage once had a bible (many probably still do), with its references to Jonah and the great whales, and some had gateways 'in the form of a Gothic arch', Nathaniel Hawthorne wrote, 'by setting up a whale's jaw bones'.[80]

Eighty years after Melville sailed on the *Acushnet*, George Francis Dow visited a New Bedford empty of sails:

> Only in one way does the past come back to us and that way, curiously enough, is through the sense of smell. The

A *wahinee*, or Hawai'ian woman, engraved by the scrimshander George Hilliot in the 1840s. And on the reverse, a New England woman, perhaps waiting back home in her parlour.

tiers of barrels of whale oil, covered with sea weed, as was the custom, formerly occupied much space on the wharves and more or less of the oil would seep out through the cracks in the barrels, and permeate the timbers and the soil on the wharves. The odor is still strong. Like the odor of the mignonette shut between the leaves of a favorite old book, it recalls the past.[81]

This may be the only time that the smell of whale has been compared to a flower.

5 A Diving Mammal

In the whaling literature before the twentieth century, a whale was often considered to be a great fish, a leviathan or monster of the deep. Yet many cultures, and some early zoologists, saw the distinction between whales and the fish they superficially resembled. In his grand *Historia animalium*, Aristotle considered dolphins and whales to have the 'oddest condition of all animals', difficult to classify because they lived as water animals, but took in air and had live births, as land animals do.[1] The Romans also recognized that whales, dolphins and seals were unique among aquatic animals: they suckled their young like mammals. For the Inuit, the god Sedna was the progenitor of marine mammals, but not of fish or birds. The culture was entirely dependent on her descendants.

The eighteenth-century Swedish naturalist Carl von Linné (Carolus Linnaeus) is generally credited with permanently extracting the whales from the fish. In his *Systema naturae*, he noted that whales have a warm bilocular heart, lungs, movable eyelids, hollow ears and, most tellingly, mammary glands. Despite their complete adaptation to the marine environment, they were not put together like fish at all. But for many years, most people still considered whales fish. In the nineteenth century, the comparative anatomist Georges Cuvier had a strong influence on the scientific view of whales, revealing their mammalian body plan.

Conrad Gesner's image *c.* 1560 of a whale and calf being attacked by an orca is one of the earliest renditions of a nursing whale.

The economist and philosopher John Stuart Mill reluctantly acknowledged that whales could be considered mammals from a zoological perspective, but he insisted that they were fish for commercial purposes: 'a plea that human laws which mention fish do not apply to whales, would be rejected at once by an intelligent judge'.[2] This would not be the last time that economic interests clashed with biological findings.

To Melville, or at least to the men aboard the *Pequod*, a whale was 'a spouting fish with a horizontal tail'.[3] The confusion persisted throughout the nineteenth century. The Arctic explorer Charles Francis Hall was familiar with the dangers of the blue whale and with the attractions of the rights and bowheads, but he was not sure of their relationship to other animals:

> I had a fine view of these monsters of the deep, as they came within a pistol-shot of the vessel. It was a grand sight to me to see a fish (is a whale a fish?) 100 feet long propelling itself quietly forward through the water as though it were but an humble mountain trout.[4]

A century later, there was still what was termed a whale

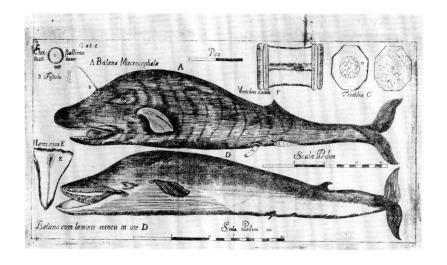

'fishery', though it was understood to mean a hunt, not a scientific error. The battles over classification between scientists and commercial interests were minor, however, compared to the flare-ups over whaling that would occur in the twentieth century. In the meantime, the two got very cozy.

Most early scientific treatises on whales, such as Robert Sibbald's *Phalanologia nova*, published in 1692, depended on strandings for their observations and measurements, and broadsides were essential to seventeenth- and eighteenth-century studies of whales. In the nineteenth century whale-ships became important platforms for scientific research. William Scoresby's *Account of the Arctic Regions with a History and Description of the Northern Whale Fishery* of 1820 was one of the earliest attempts by a whaling captain to record the life history of his quarry, in this case the bowhead.

A few physicians and surgeons aboard whale-ships, with more free time than the crew, kept close observational records

The 17th-century depictions of whales by the Scottish physician Robert Sibbald are among the earliest accurate renditions of cetaceans.

Frontispiece to Thomas Beale's *Natural History of the Sperm Whale* (1839).

of whales and whaling techniques. These studies emerged from the medical tradition, the careful observation of the human body and its actions. The British surgeon Thomas Beale published his ground-breaking *The Natural History of the Sperm Whale* in 1835; it was the first full description of the sperm whale, which until that time was little understood beyond the gunwales of a whaleboat or the blubber room of a whale-ship.

Charles Scammon was a successful nineteenth-century whaling captain on the west coast of North America. Although he published only one book and one technical paper, he would come to have influence on the field of cetology. Along with *Moby-Dick*, Scammon's *The Marine Mammals of the Northwestern Coast of North America, Together with an Account of the American Whale-Fishery* (1874) is considered to be one of the greatest books ever written about whales and whaling. A dedicated whaler and scientist, he solicited measurements and samples from his whaling acquaintances and began collecting data – including the length, girth, thickness and colour of blubber, and the number of baleen plates – on every marine mammal species available to him. Later scientific research conducted aboard whale-ships was indebted to his work.

As a whaler, Scammon pursued the Pacific grey whale, which he hunted along the coast of California, 'a pleasant retreat from the rough voyages experienced in the whale-ship'.[5] Although commercial whaling of this species began in 1795, when John Locke started hunting the coastal 'scrags' in a British whaler, Scammon is generally credited with (or blamed for) discovering the breeding grounds in Laguna Ojo de Liebra in Baja California. Females and calves were the initial focus of the hunt. But, with the development of a shoulder-launched harpoon, or bomb gun, in the nineteenth century, 'kelp whaling' began along the grey whale's migratory route. Whalers anchored their boats in the kelp beds, within a few kilometres of the shore, waiting for grey whales to approach; on sight of a whale, they would scull into its trajectory so that the gunner could get a close shot. According to Scammon, 'the keen-eyed "Devil-fish"' soon learned the

A wood engraving from *Harper's Weekly* of a whaling station on the California coast, 1877. Note the look-out, top left.

consequence of getting too near 'the long, dark-looking object . . . rising and falling with the rolling swell'. The whales, and then the whalers, moved offshore. By the time that Scammon published his work in 1874, most of the whales were gone: 'this peculiar branch of whaling is dying out, owing to the scarcity of the animals which now visit the coast; and even these have become exceedingly difficult to approach'.[6] One of the leading nineteenth-century cetologists had been partly responsible for the near-extinction of his study animal.

As the debate over the classification of whales died down at the end of the nineteenth century, the next question arose – what *kind* of mammals are they? Do cetaceans form a separate lineage that broke off when mammals arose in the Cretaceous, or should they be nested among other mammalian groups that had never left the land?

In 1883 the British anatomist W. H. Flower suggested that cetaceans and ungulates, or hoofed mammals, were closely related. But his was an unconventional view, and until the 1950s most evolutionary biologists believed that whales had a very ancient origin and no close relatives among other living mammals. Recent genetic and paleontological studies take Flower's assertion one step further: cetaceans *are* ungulates or artiodactyls that adapted to the sea; they are evolutionarily nested among pigs and peccaries, hippos and sheep, cows and camels.[7]

Fossil cetaceans have been unearthed around the world: prominent sites are found in Egypt, New Zealand, Patagonia, Chesapeake Bay, California and Peru. One of the oldest is *Pakicetus*, a 47-million-year-old fossil discovered in Pakistan. About the size of a coyote, this ancestor of modern whales was a marginal creature whose webbed hind legs enabled it to swim in shallow seas and move about on the shore. It was a carnivore, eating terrestrial animals and residing in streams. As with

Pakicetus was a wolf-size ancestor of whales that lived along the water's edge 47 million years ago.

modern-day manatees, *Pakicetus* had very dense bones, serving as ballast to keep the early whale from rising to the surface.

Recently another whale ancestor has been uncovered in Asia. *Rhodocetus* measured about 3 metres long, with webbed feet that it used to paddle through the water, and a metre-long tail that functioned as a rudder. (It did not wiggle its tail for propulsion in water like an otter, as palaeontologists had previously suggested.) *Rhodocetus* had reduced hind limbs, a small step towards modern whales, which have lost their rear legs entirely; only vestigial bones remain.

Such ancient fossils notwithstanding, the difference between a domestic sheep and a sperm whale does seem dauntingly vast. It is hard to imagine a common ancestor for a woolly 40-kilogram ruminant and a skilled aquatic predator that weighs up to 40,000 kilograms, dives 2,000 metres, holds its breath for 75 minutes

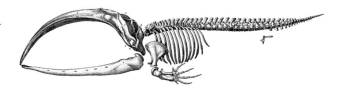

Although whales have lost their rear limbs through evolution, they retain vestigial pelvic bones, as shown beneath the tail of this bowhead whale skeleton.

and feeds on giant squid. With a gap this wide, creationists have used the origin of whales as an example of why evolution is impossible.[8]

Yet the DNA and fossil record show that all modern whales, both the toothed and baleen, descend from these ancient cetaceans. For years, it was thought that pigs were the closest living relatives to whales. Using DNA analysis, though, Japanese biologists have revealed that the hippopotamus is their sister group. Aquatic mammals themselves, hippos lack hair and sweat glands, barely break the surface of the water to breathe, and can communicate underwater. Like sperm whales and other cetaceans, male hippopotamuses use head-to-head open-mouth charges to challenge opponents, followed by a shoving contest.[9] The similarities were long considered convergent, that is, separate adaptations to life underwater. It now seems that these behaviours evolved deep in the past, before hippos split from whales.

Today there are considered to be fourteen species of great whales, although such designations are still in flux. The monsters of the Middle Ages may have been put to rest, but molecular researchers are discovering new whales in familiar forms. The northern right whale, for example, was once considered a single species, with a range stretching from the Bay of Biscay to Japan. DNA analysis tells us that the populations of the Pacific and Atlantic have been separated for millions of years. In Japan, biologists claim that the sei whale may actually consist of two separate species, swimming side by side, but never interbreeding.

The excellent *Encyclopædia of Marine Mammals*, published in 2002, provides guidance, if not firm answers, to questions on whale systematics, anatomy and human impacts. Yet controversies of classification are likely to rage on for years among marine mammal taxonomists. Depending on whom you ask, there are about 70 to 80 species of cetaceans, divided at present into nine families. All of the great whales but one are mysticetes or baleen whales, which form a single evolutionary lineage. Mysticete is from the Greek *mystax*, or moustache, for the horny, keratinous plates, arranged in rows, that filter fish and crustaceans from seawater.

There are four families of baleen whales. The Balaenidae or right whales include the North Atlantic right whale, North Pacific right whale, southern right whale and the Arctic bowhead. These whales, the first to be hunted commercially, are now among the most endangered of cetaceans. There are about 350 right whales in the North Atlantic, and probably fewer in the North Pacific. In *Moby-Dick*, Melville compared the shape of their head to a shoemaker's last, a shoe in which 'that old woman of the nursery tale, with the swarming brood, might very comfortably be lodged'.[10]

Both the Neobalaenidae and Eschrictiidae are monotypic – they are represented by a single extant species. The pygmy right whale, the only neobalaenid, is little studied and rarely exploited. A fully grown pygmy is about the size of a right-whale calf. *Eschrictius robustus*, the grey whale, or scrag whale, is found only in the Pacific, although North Atlantic grey whales existed at least until the eighteenth century.

The rorqual whales, or Balaenopteridae, include the common minke whale, Antarctic minke whale, sei whale, Bryde's whale, blue whale, fin whale and humpback whale. The word *rorqual*, from the Norwegian *rörhval*, means grooved whale – all rorquals have long pleats on the underside of the throat that run about three-quarters of the length of their body. These pleats enable the whale to extend its throat when taking in small prey – krill and schooling fish such as herring. The hairy fringes of the baleen plates capture food as water is expelled.

The sperm whale is a toothed whale, or odontocete, a relative of beaked whales and bottlenose dolphins. Although most of the 70 or so species of toothed whales are much smaller than the mysticetes, the size of sperm whales (bulls can reach 18 metres in length and weigh 50 tonnes) and their essential role in the history of whaling argues for their inclusion in a cultural, if not evolutionary, history of great whales.

In leaving dry land behind, whales were no longer restricted by the limits of gravity. Their limbs did not have to support their weight, and organs were suspended in the body cavity. Living a buoyant life, they grew enormous. A full-grown male blue whale is 25 metres long. Females often reach 30 metres, close to the length of a Boeing 737.[11] At birth, they are the size of a whaleboat; fully grown, they would be almost the size of the ships themselves. Such body size is a critical adaptation for a warm-blooded animal in a cold sea. In the ocean, heat is dissipated much more rapidly than it is on land. A bigger animal has a smaller proportion of its body exposed to the environment. Even the smallest marine mammals are quite a bit larger than their terrestrial relatives. There are no sea mice or marine shrews; only the otter, with its thick fur, has managed to colonize the sea successfully. Most sea mammals are hairless, large and full of fat.

Blubber, the vascularized layer of adipose tissue just beneath the skin, is essential in maintaining this level of warmth. Arctic bowheads have the thickest blubber, a 50-centimetre layer of fat. Comprising up to half the body mass of some whales, blubber is

A whale skeleton reassembled between *c.* 1900 and *c.* 1930.

more than an insulator: it is the primary site of energy storage, critical to an animal that may fast for up to half the year.

Unique to marine mammals, blubber forms a continuous layer of fat across the body of a whale, lying just above the muscles. Adipocytes, or fat cells, swell with lipids as the whale feeds, and then empty during the long winter fast. The metabolism of fat provides energy and water to the fasting whale: a kilogram of water is released for every kilogram of lipid burned. Besides these fat cells, blubber is rich in collagen, giving it strength and pliability, and blood vessels, important in regulating temperature.[12] Blubber streamlines the whale, serving as an elastic spring when diving.[13]

Humpback, right and sperm whales fluke – their tails rising above the water – when they sound; this motion provides vertical thrust for these buoyant, sometimes deep-diving whales.

William Scoresby's 1820 description of the Arctic whale fishery was one of the earliest natural histories written by a whaling captain. This plate illustrates the diverse planktonic prey of his quarry. Bowheads mostly survive on krill and copepods, the crustacean with long antennae at bottom right.

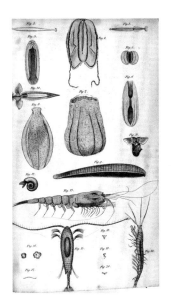

Leaving behind access to oxygen, whales store this essential molecule in their blood and muscle; only 10 per cent is retained in the lungs of sperm whales when they dive. The storage of oxygen in muscles enables them to descend more than 2 kilometres, the deepest dives of any mammal.[14]

What do whales really eat? The common answer is plankton – zooplankton, to be exact, which can be any animal adrift in the sea, from protozoa to vertebrates. Most baleen whales are catholic feeders. In the North Pacific and Bering Sea, six species of krill, four species of copepods, one species of the sand-burrowing amphipod, one species of mysid shrimp, two species of crabs, ten species of fish and more than one squid species have been found in the belly of baleen whales.[15]

In the North Atlantic, one of the most common planktonic species eaten by rorqual whales is *Meganyctiphanes norvegica*, or northern krill. A staple in the krill's diet also comprises most of the food consumed by the northern right whale: both the 3-centimetre crustacean and the 50-tonne cetacean depend on large populations of *Calanus finmarchicus*, the copepod, to survive.

In his essay of 1725 on the whales of New England, Paul Dudley noted that the right whale's throat

> is not much bigger than an Ox's, but the Finback Whale has a larger Swallow: for he lives upon smaller Fish, as Mackeral, Hering, &c. great [Schools] of which they run through, and, with a short Turn, cause an Eddy or Whirlpool, by the Force of which, the small Fish are brought into a Cluster; so that this Fish, with open Mouth, will take some Hundreds of them at a time.[16]

Krill emptying from the belly of a whale onto the deck of a factory ship.

It was an amazing observation for 1725. And although fin whales may not create a whirlpool, they do encircle schools, using their white bellies as a wall, and then rush in with their enormous gape, much as modern purse seiners circle schools of herring or mackerel and then vacuum their prey into the hold.

One of the most sophisticated styles of hunting is that of the humpback. Blowing bubbles beneath a school of fish such as herring, the whale causes the school to cluster tightly and then rises in the bubble net to scoop up a huge mouthful of food. The most legendary battles are between sperm whales and squid, a struggle that can be read in the scars on sperm whales from the giant squid's tentacles. Bullen described a conflict between these giants that he saw on night watch in the Indian Ocean:

> Getting the night-glasses out of the cabin scuttle . . . I focused them on the troubled spot, perfectly satisfied by a short examination that neither volcano nor earthquake had anything to do with what was going on . . . A very large sperm whale was locked in deadly conflict with a cuttle-fish, or squid, almost as large as himself, whose interminable tentacles seemed to enlace the whole of his great body. The head of the whale especially seemed a perfect net-work of writhing arms – naturally, I suppose, for it appeared as if the whale had the tail part of the mollusc in his jaws, and, in a business-like, methodical way, was sawing through it. By the side of the black columnar head of the whale appeared the head of the great squid, as awful an object as one could well imagine even in a fevered dream. . . . The eyes were very remarkable from their size and blackness, which contrasted with the livid whiteness of the head. . . . All around the combatants were numerous sharks, like jackals around a lion, ready to share the feast.[17]

Cetaceans, along with manatees and hippos, are the only mammals that give birth underwater. Whale embryos may disclose their onshore origins: a cetacean fetus has legs, nostrils on the tip of the snout and genitals outside the body surface. But when the hind limbs disappear, the nostrils migrate to blowholes atop the head and the genitals retreat behind a slit, streamlining the body and keeping the reproductive organs warm, the whale emerges.

After birth, young whales stay close to their mothers, making frequent body contact and sometimes riding on top of the mother's flukes. Watching a calf at sea is one of the best opportunities to observe whales. During a research voyage in the Gulf Stream off Florida, some colleagues and I tracked a right-whale mother and calf. For hours the calf circled its mother, occasionally spy-hopping – lifting its shoe-shaped head above the surface and looking at the airy world above – and then resting on its mother's back. A Bonaparte gull swam in and alighted on the mother's flanks as she minded her calf. The youngest whales are also the most curious; it is not unusual for a juvenile whale to approach a research vessel and eye its crew, before the mother calls it back.

Despite the scepticism among whalers as to the mammalian origins of their quarry, they understood one feature common to mammals: the maternal bond. Calves are slow, easily seen and offer little resistance to the harpoon. And they spend lots of time feeding. Humpback calves drink up to 450 litres – four barrels – of milk a day.[18] In the Caribbean, humpback cow-calf pairs were the prey of choice for traditional and modern whalers. In the search for right whales, the whale biologist E. A. Wilson noted in 1907: 'the hunt began with the destruction of the calf . . . because it was known that the mother would then become easy prey, as she would not leave the bay without her suckling'. This type of whaling was perhaps 'the most complete and rapid method of exterminating an animal that has ever been adopted'.[19]

Female baleen whales are larger than males, enabling them to store the tremendous amounts of energy needed to carry a foetus to term and then nurse the multi-tonne offspring through the long winter fast.[20] Whalers, intent on the largest animals, were familiar with the reproductive cycles of whales. Pregnant females had huge stores of fat and were highly desirable. After weaning their calves, the 'dry skins' were worth little to whalers.

Whalers recorded that female bowhead, right, humpback and fin whales would brave injury or sacrifice their life for their calves. But for one species, the killing of a calf proved dangerous. To whalers, grey whales were the devilfish – when their calves were attacked, the enraged cows would respond by overturning the boats and killing the hunters. The whalers were quick learners. Instead of leaving the lagoon, they would turn their harpoons on the mother. An orphaned calf was easy prey.

In contrast, the hunt for sperm whales focused on large bulls, which yielded greater quantities of oil. Melville saw the bull whale – half as long again as the female, as the 'harem's lord'.[21] After years of observation at sea, the Canadian biologist Hal Whitehead suggested that associations between males and females were actually regulated by mutual consent, perhaps mediated by the presence of other large males in the area.[22]

For millions of years the social nature of sperm whales served them well. Females live in clans, enabling them to babysit each other's calves. Young whales, tethered to the surface by a small lung capacity, cannot be left alone during the long dives taken by adults in search of benthic fish and large deepwater squid. So females take turns in minding the infants: they nurse communally – there are almost always more lactating females than there are calves in a clan – and keep vigil for predators such as sharks and killer whales.[23]

Yet the exploitation of females can result in the death of an entire clan, since an attack on a calf or a matriarch might attract the entire group to come to her aid. When threatened, sperm whales often gather in a circle, thrashing their flukes on the outer edge of the ring. This defence, which one Japanese researcher described as a marguerite flower or daisy, might work against orcas, but modern whalers intentionally harpooned the largest whale in a group, hoping to prompt the formation of a marguerite. The hunters then plucked the whales from the sea, petal by petal.[24]

The distances between feeding and breeding areas may be enormous. In the Northern Hemisphere, some humpbacks migrate from Iceland to the Caribbean each winter; in the Southern, from the Antarctic to Colombia. Grey whales make the longest migration of any mammal on the planet, almost 20,000 kilometres from the Bering Sea to Baja California and back each year.

As they approach the breeding grounds, male humpbacks start to sing and fin-whale sperm counts begin to rise. As one might expect from the largest animals on the planet, the details are humbling. In the sixteenth century, the French naturalist Guillaume Rondelet wrote:

> Since mating whales cannot unite at close quarters due to their huge bodies, their membrum virile is 13 cubits long. Once I saw a whale organ that size slung over the shoulder of a tall man, with both ends dragging on the ground. You can imagine how big it must get when whales anxious to mate are in pursuit of females.[25]

Although the length of the whale penis does not approach 13 cubits (more than 6 metres) and is not extensible, the 2.5-metre penis of the right whale can be moved with the dexterity of a very large finger. Unlike sperm whales, which use their enormous heads and spermaceti organs to defeat their opponents, right whales compete with genitalia and sperm. In a group that may include up to 30 suitors, males will follow a female for hours with each intromission an attempt to dilute the sperm of the previous encounters. The one-tonne testes are the size of washing machines.

Whales were attractive to humans because of the very adaptations that make them so successful in the oceans. Their enormous size made an individual animal a feast for an entire village, spurring trade between communities. The maternal bond enabled whalers to double their catch, and reproductive groups allowed them to increase it by an order of magnitude. The very breath of a whale could put it in the way of a harpoon.

The migration of nostrils to the top of the head enabled cetaceans to breathe without surfacing; only the blowholes and a sliver of the body emerge when a whale respires. The lung capacity of whales is enormous; an adult blue whale can inhale 5,000 litres, a room full of air, before sounding.[26]

The rapid exhalation, visible because of the vapour and sea water entrained into a column of air, was seen by the shore-based observer and from the mast aloft. Whether it was in the form of a coded message from a *vigía* or a call of 'She blows!', the response was relentless.

6 Oil and Bone

Whales and fire. Among some Arctic peoples, the whale captain's wife was required to keep the fire in the home burning until the hunt was over. She also had to stay in her tent and allow no visitors to be received until the whales were captured or had escaped (perhaps in an attempt to prevent a different kind of fire from catching flame).[1] In Europe and Asia, there were the tales of Brendan and of Sinbad who lit fires on the back of sleeping whales. In China, ambergris was dragon spittle. For Ahab, the 'white forked flame' is the whale. Moby Dick and 'God's burning finger', the lightning above the *Pequod*, both command the same degree of reverence: 'Oh! thou clear spirit of clear fire, whom on these seas I as Persian once did worship . . . I now know that thy right worship is defiance.'[2]

In Walt Disney's *Pinocchio*, (1940) the brave puppet rescues his father Geppetto and himself by lighting a fire in the belly of a whale. Monstro – 'a whale of a whale', according to Jiminy Cricket, who 'swallows whole ships alive' – swims in the tradition of Sinbad's angry whale, a danger to all those at sea. A sullen lump of blubber with a glutinous scowl, the fanciful Monstro is part rorqual, part sperm, part Jonah motif and all Disney. The whale is a submarine prison, with a cavern of air supplied by the monster. In Carlo Lorenzini's *Adventures of Pinocchio*, written in 1882, Geppetto and Pinocchio are swallowed by a dogfish.

Rather than lighting a fire, they escape the monster while he sleeps.

The association of whales and fire may run through many cultures, but, to the whale, the real risk of the flame, of course, was the oil field just beneath its skin. The commercial rendering of clean-burning oil from whale blubber drastically changed the relationship between cetaceans and humans. 'It is by reason of this cosy blanketing of his body', Melville wrote, 'that the whale is enabled to keep himself comfortable in all weathers, in all seas, times, and tides.'[3] This blanket did keep whales comfortable, but it also made them highly profitable. To Yankee whalers, a blanket was a 500-kilogram strip of blubber.

At first, right whales supplied whale or 'train' oil. Whale oil contains glycerides from fatty acids – a fat derived from blubber, which is identical to compounds in human fat. The oil was used for lighting, for lubrication and for cleansing in the form of soft soaps.

Casks of sperm oil on a New Bedford wharf. The oil rendered from whale blubber was central to the relationship between humans and cetaceans for centuries.

118

In the eighteenth and nineteenth centuries, sperm oil replaced whale oil. Unlike the glycerides found in baleen whale oil, sperm whales and other odontocetes store a long-chained molecule known as a wax ester. Composed of alcohol and fatty acids, these waxes are stable, clean burning and resist degradation. Sperm oil soon became the illuminant of choice, a superior product to replace declining whale-oil stocks.[4] As a bonus to whale men, the spermaceti, which filled the enormous head, made the world's finest candles. Spermaceti, from the Latin *sperma*, for semen or sperm, and *cetus*, for sea monster or whale, is an early English misconception that continues to this day. The confusion is understandable; when spermaceti crystallizes it is reported to look like mammalian ejaculate, and, according to the biologist Richard Laws, 'Anyone who has seen a sperm whale's case cut open knows that spermaceti has a strong smell of semen.'[5] The spermaceti organ may not produce sperm, but in conjunction with the junk, air sacs and clapper system at the front of the sperm whale's head, it helps to form and focus the whale's click with which it echolocates its prey and communicates within family units.[6] And it does play a role in reproduction – bull whales battle for females with their heads.

As the whalers established contact with islanders throughout the Pacific, they were followed by missionaries. The whaler and writer Nathan Cole Haley noted that the priest on Rotumah had 'instructed some and made a little reform in their morals, with still a big field left for him to work during his spare time'.[7] The Roman Catholic Church adapted to the move: until it established parishes in the South Pacific all liturgical candles had to be made of beeswax. A papal disposition was given to parishes visited by whalers in the Southern Hemisphere.[8] With beeswax hard to come by, spermaceti candles were permitted on altars close to the whaling grounds and far from Rome.

Although whale populations typically increased during wartime – when mariners were preoccupied with destroying each other rather than killing whales – seasonal harvests in the Southern Hemisphere rose to more than 11,000 whales per year during the First World War. The goal of the hunt was glycerine, a by-product of the hydrogenation of whale oil, which solidified it into edible margarine. This syrupy alcohol was the primary component in the manufacture of nitroglycerine, essential to making dynamite for the war and useful in cardiology. Whaling gunners were encouraged to kill whale after whale in the quest for glycerine, even when no factory was in sight.[9]

In the thirteenth-century *King's Mirror*, baleen was believed to cause the death of whales, preventing them from closing their mouths. The French surgeon Ambroise Paré proposed in his sixteenth-century treatise on monsters that baleen functioned like whiskers, 'so that the whale will not bump against the rocks'.[10] Paul Dudley was one of the first to get it right in 1725: ''Tis thought by some, that the hairy Part of the Whale-bone, and which is next to the Tongue, serves in the Nature of a Strainer of their Food.' Once again ahead of his time, Dudley also noted the similarities between whales and hoofed mammals: 'The Entrails of this Whale are made and situated much like those of an Ox.'[11]

The foetuses of both baleen and toothed whales have tooth buds. Baleen whale embryos, however, reabsorb the buds before birth, developing longitudinal ridges on their upper jaw composed of epidermal folds. These folds become cornified and develop into the keratinous baleen plates.

The Inuit recognized the similarity of baleen and our own keratinous adaptations: in some versions, the origin of baleen was Sedna's fingernails. As with our nails, the relative thickness of the baleen plates can be used to assess the nutritional state of a whale: the alternating summer feast and winter fast in most whales leaves growth zones not unlike rings on a tree. You cannot easily tell the age of a whale this way, since the plates wear down after five or six years.[12]

Baleen, or whalebone, was found in every corner of the home: skirt hoops, tongue scrapers, shoehorns, fishing rods, divining rods, canes and riding whips. The finer fringes were used in brooms and flue brushes. Blubber may have lit the world, but the most significant baleen product was usually kept in the dark: the whalebone corset was designed to give fashionable women the smallest waist possible. Baleen rods were first employed to crimp the waists of young girls in England during the reign of Mary Tudor. Not to be outdone in the realm of the waistline, Catherine de Médicis, Queen of France, declared the ideal waist size to be 13 inches.[13]

Stiff busks, often sawed from sperm-whale jawbones in the nineteenth century, were inserted in the front of the corset to ensure erect posture. On ships, whalers carved elaborate patterns on these bones; it would be hard to imagine a more intimate gift for a loved one after years at sea.

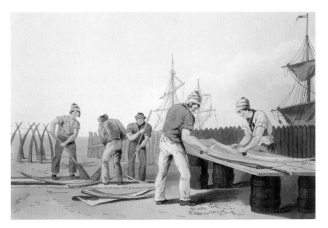

Preparing whalebone, or baleen, in Yorkshire, 1813.

In the 19th century there were whalebone corsets for summer, corsets for winter, corsets for every shape and size. The corset on the lower left was designed for a child between 1 and 2 years old.

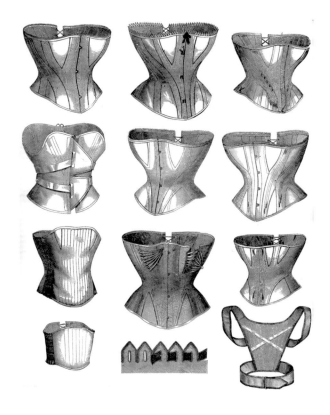

So restrictive were these bodices that the eighteenth-century French physician Nicholas Andry recommended their use to cure scoliosis, the curvature of the spine. Women paid the price of keeping waists as thin as a supermodel's thigh: rib cages became deformed and some women had to have their floating ribs removed. Yet corsets were more than a fashionable assault on the body: they restored a youthful figure to the middle aged and gave an air of aristocracy to the middle classes. The practice of wearing corsets continued for centuries. In 1853, at

Fashionable women relied on whalebone to hone an hourglass figure. These seaside summer outfits had all the lacing and tight boning of normal dresses.

Baleen from bowhead whales drying on wharves at the Arctic Oil Works in San Francisco.

the peak of Yankee whaling, 5,652,300 lb of baleen were landed at US ports, with a value of $1,950,000.[14]

Whalebone was not only a source of pain for women; it was also used to discipline wild schoolchildren – when a child was struck with a whalebone whip, he got a 'whaling'. In *Uncle Tom's Cabin*, Simon Legree lashes his slave with his riding whip and taunts, 'How did yer like yer whaling, Tom?'[15] By the late twentieth century, the verb had been cut loose of its keratinous origins, though a whipping was still a whaling and the poet still 'whaled away at his critics'.[16]

The magnitude of the whale had its advantages when it came to hyperbole. A comparison to a whale could be a larger-than-life compliment, J. B. Priestley wrote in 1954: 'An equally dashing, whale-of-a-fellow, RAF type'. One could also be 'a whale in geography', or better, have 'a whale of a good time'.[17]

Of all the products of whales, ambergris was the most exotic and highly prized. It has been valued as an aphrodisiac, laxative, spice and for incense and cosmetics. Egyptians poured coffee oveer melted ambergris to flavour their brew. In China, it was a rare luxury, worth its weight in gold. Chinese merchants sold it as a product of the western sea of the Romans, where dragons were found in large numbers. 'When a dragon is lying on a rock asleep, his spittle floats on the water, collects and turns hard, and the fishermen gather it as a most valuable substance.'[18] In the West, ambergris was the dung or sperm of whales and, in the Middle East, it was solidified sea spray; a deep-sea fungus, as prized as truffles on land; or beeswax run into the sea.[19]

The Flemish botanist Carolus Clusius wrote the first description of the true source of ambergris, the intestines of a whale, in 1574. After the rise of the Yankee whale fishery, it was recognized that only the deep-water sperm whales produced the expensive product, which became highly valued as a fixative for fragrances in perfume. Although the beaks of squid are often found within lumps of ambergris, the cause of its formation remains unknown. It is found in less than 5 per cent of whales.[20] The concretions are usually less than 10 kilograms, though one of the largest on record is 420 kilograms;[21] it required a crane to remove it from a bull sperm whale in the Southern Ocean in 1953.

Although beachcombers may find mysterious globs ashore, the whale biologist Dale Rice has noted that ambergris is rarely recovered without a whale carcass. He suggests this test to confirm the identity of a seaside clump:

> heat a wire or needle in a flame and thrust it into a sample to a depth of about a centimeter; if the substance is really ambergris it will instantly melt into an opaque fluid the color of dark chocolate. When the needle is withdrawn, the ambergris will leave a tacky residue on it.[22]

Fresh ambergris smells like whale faeces, a pungent stench that mellows with age. Its odour has been compared to that of a fine cigar. The whaling chemist Christopher Ash wrote that it reminded him of 'a cool English wood in spring, and the scent you smell when you tear up the moss to uncover the dark soil underneath'.[23]

'Positively Real Whale': for those who never boarded a whale ship, carcasses transported by railroad cars might provide the only chance to see – and smell – a real whale.

Human wars were often welcome respites for cetaceans. During the American Civil War, the Confederate captain James Waddell attacked the Yankee whaling fleet, capturing and burning ships from Dakar to Australia and the Arctic. His sailing ship, built in Britain, had auxiliary steam power that enabled him to overtake slow-moving whalers. To his credit, he never killed a man in his exploits, safely delivering Yankee crews to the nearest port. Confederate raiders destroyed 40 whale-ships, and 40 more were sunk to block harbours in the South.

The Yankee whale fishery never recovered. With so many ships lost, there was a chance for owners to modernize their fleet after the war. But they never embraced the new technologies. On top of that, petroleum had been discovered in Pennsylvania in 1859. Surprisingly, this cheap alternative fuel had the same ultimate source as whale oil – plankton – even if, in the case of petroleum, the plankton was fossilized. The price of whale oil, which peaked at $1.45 per US gallon in 1865, was down to 31 cents in 1905. The industry's first response to falling prices was to hunt more whales.

Although women were stuffed into hourglass corsets until the end of the nineteenth century, standards were loosening. Ferris Good Sense Corset Waists, 'made after the natural beauty of the human form', became popular. As the wasp waist passed from fashion, so did the need to waste money on whalebone in an attempt to achieve an almost inhuman form. The retail price of baleen fell from $5 to 50 cents per pound. Spring steel was introduced in 1907, quickly replacing baleen as a more flexible and cheaper material.

The advent of fossil fuels and spring steel, along with changing fashions, might have been the death knoll for commercial whaling. Instead, cannons, petroleum and new industrial products opened the hunt for an entirely different group of whales.

7 Floating Factories

In antiquity, whaling was a small-scale operation, with rich pre-historic roots in the Arctic. Pelagic whaling and other developments helped to change the approach that humans had to cetaceans, enabling a whale to be killed and processed without returning to shore. But the 1860s marked a watershed in whaling technology, a division so deep that some historians divide whaling into the old and modern traditions at this time.

At this time, the Norwegian sealer Svend Foyn and the American Thomas Roys were working independently on explosive harpoons. Roys patented his shoulder-mounted gun in 1861. He insisted that the device 'invariably fastens to Whales at distances of 100 feet, and at the explosion of the shell, eight seconds after gives instant death'. Death may not have been instant, but Roys's prediction – that new technology would 'prove the Whaling business in its infancy' – was dead on.[1]

It was Foyn's bow-mounted cannon that became the industry standard. In 1863 he killed a blue whale, the leviathan, using a one-tonne cannon mounted on a steamship. The one-metre, diamond-shaped harpoon had a fragmentation bomb at its tip, which exploded when it penetrated the whale. The attached cable was then winched back to the ship by steam power, bringing the dying whale with it. Leviathans, the British marine biologist Alister Hardy noted, 'can now be caught and pulled in like

The *Nancy Grey*, a whale catcher, with its quarry off Skacro, Norway, c. 1890.

fish on a line'.[2] The harpoon was strong enough for a sinking whale to be pulled to the surface, where compressed air was injected into the carcass.

Suddenly every species on the globe was open to exploitation. Before the innovation of the harpoon grenade, living blue whales were too swift and dead blues sank too quickly to be hunted efficiently. With the arrival of new technology, they would become the standard against which all other whales were compared. The largest animal ever captured was a female blue whale taken off South Georgia; she was 33 metres long with an estimated weight of 190 tonnes. Yet even an average blue whale is considerable: adult body weights range from 80 to 150 tonnes. Their blood vessels are so large that a full-grown trout could swim through them.[3] Even their blows are enormous,

128

reaching 9 metres into the sky. These long, slender spouts made them all the more visible to hunters. The rise of industrial whaling coincided with the discovery of the richest whaling grounds on Earth.[4] In 1904 the Norwegian whaler C. F. Larsen, arriving at the South Atlantic island of South Georgia, reported on the blues, fins, humpbacks and right whales he saw: 'I saw them in hundreds and thousands.'[5] Although he had trouble raising money in Europe, Larsen established a whaling station on the island with funds raised in Argentina. It was an instant success; within the decade, eight whaling stations opened on South Georgia. More than 18,000 humpbacks were taken in the first ten years, and about 40,000 blues were killed within the first three decades of commercial operation. The populations crashed and have never recovered.[6]

Innovations did not stop with the harpoon gun. In 1924 the Norwegian gunner Petter Sørlle of Vestfeld invented the stern slipway. Using hydraulic tail grabbers, entire whales could be winched onto the flensing deck, where enormous pressure cookers were used to process the animals. In the 1850s it took

Dead rorqual whales inflated with compressed air for transport to a factory ship, c. 1935–45.

about 36 hours to render an adult sperm whale. By the 1920s even the largest males could be processed in less than one.[7] The barrel-shaped casks that once lined the wharves were replaced with vast tanks in the hull of the ship. The wooden cask – the symbol of whaling for centuries – disappeared.

The 13,246-tonne *C. F. Larsen* was fitted out in Norway in 1926. A news account noted: 'This is the largest ship hitherto employed in the service of whaling, and there is a strong possibility that the limit has been reached.'[8] These factory ships helped to open up the southern oceans to exploitation. In 1914 about half of the world's whale oil came from the Antarctic. By 1938, 92 per cent was coming from the south.[9] The size of the *Larsen* was exceeded in just a few years, and by the 1960s the *average* floating factory was more than 19,000 tonnes.

Whale catchers, often the size of nineteenth-century whale-ships, were employed to do the killing. Equipped with grenade harpoons, early catchers used steam power to track their prey

A blanket of blubber is removed from a rorqual whale carcass, c. 1935–45.

and tow carcasses. Diesel engines were introduced into the industry in the 1930s. At first whalers resisted the new technology, believing that the tremendous noise of a diesel engine would frighten the whales. They were right. In the time of oars and sail, and even in the age of steam, whalers could sneak up and surprise an unsuspecting animal. The catcher was compelled to chase down its prey and tire it before shooting.

A Japanese whaler, the *Yushin Maru*, harpoons a whale in the Southern Ocean, *c.* 2001–2.

As hunting changed, so did the use of whale oil – from fuel source to food. Although edible, the oil has a strong smell, considered distasteful by most Westerners. With the development of hydrogenation – in which two hydrogen atoms are added to oleic acid, the most common fatty acid in whale oil – a solid fat that was odour-free was produced: margarine. Developed for beef fat in the nineteenth century, hydrogenation began on an industrial scale around 1909. Whale-oil production increased quickly.[10]

Thumbing through images of factory whaling is a grim experience, like a tour of a slaughterhouse. Gone is that force of nature that terrified nineteenth-century greenhands. Even eagle-eyed whalers were no longer essential to spot a blow: spotter planes were flown in to follow the trail of hunted whales. The catcher boats were highly efficient. The Canadian writer Farley Mowat described a boat off the coast of Canada:

> *Thoranin* was a 200-foot, 800-ton, 2,000-horsepower diesel-electric killing machine, whose 90 mm harpoon gun mounted high on her destroyer bow had already taken the lives of thousands of great whales in southern waters. She could range 300 miles from base, kill and take in tow eight or nine big whales, return them to shore, and be off again within a few hours on a new sweep of destruction.[11]

Was it this industrial-scale whaling that diminished the appeal of it as sport? There are only a few records of hunters pursuing whales for trophy. One of the earliest is from the eleventh century BC. An avid hunter of oxen, elephants and lions, the Assyrian king Tiglathpileser I considered the slaying of a sperm whale his greatest hunting achievement.[12] At the turn of the century, recreational fishing parties chased fin whales with elephant guns and swordfish harpoons. Occasionally a sportsman would even board a whaler. In 1905 the British naturalist J. G. Millais described his experience aboard a Norwegian whaler hunting fin whales off Newfoundland:

> There was a feeling of intense exhilaration as we rushed northwards, the spray flying from our bows as the ship leapt from crest to crest in the heavy swell. I have enjoyed the rushes of gallant thirty- and even forty-pound salmon

in heavy water on the Tay, the supreme moments in an angler's life, but that was mere child's play to the intense excitement which we now experienced during the next three hours. To be in tow of a wild whale is something to experience and remember to one's dying day. You feel that you are alive, and that you are there with the sport of kings.[13]

But the sport never really caught on. Unlike shark fishing, which attracted recreational fishermen in the twentieth century, there were no whale tournaments – perhaps because whales cannot be fished with bait. Or was it that whale hunting was inexorably associated with the stinkeries, try-works and floating factories?

Whalers sometimes expressed remorse for their actions. A Scottish gunner, who claimed to have killed 2,000 whales, told Mowat:

We never wanted to know too much about them . . . It was too much like murder as it was. I think if I'd had the Celtic gift of 'sight' and could have looked into the minds of these beasts, I'd have had to give up the sea and go ashore for good. There're times when too much knowledge can stand in a man's way.[14]

The British zoologist F. D. Ommanney described the death of a whale harpooned from a catcher boat. At 500 metres distance, from a deck several metres above the surface of the sea, the whalers are at a remove from their prey:

If whales could utter cries which could rend the heart, deaths would be less dreadful than this losing battle which our whale was now engaged upon in silence broken only by the far-off screaming of sea birds. We could not even hear the thrashing of crimson foam as he writhed and plunged, spouting a bloody spray at first, then an upgushing, followed by a bubbling upwelling amid a spreading island of blood . . . the struggle ceased, the red foam subsided and we could see the body lying quite still. The birds busied themselves above and around it with shrill cries.[15]

As in the American Civil War, there was a brief respite in the hunt for whales during the Second World War. Floating factories were converted to tankers, the enormous flensing decks carrying materials that were too large to transport by most carriers. German whale chasers were used to hunt for submarines and sweep for mines. In 1941 the Japanese launched miniature submarines from the slipways of whaling ships to attack Pearl Harbor.[16] With the hunt suspended, mineral oil was used instead of whale oil whenever possible.

This might have saved some whales from the hunt in the Southern Hemisphere, but Mowat contends that, with depth charges and bombs, 'tens of thousands of whales were killed by the men who hunted submarines with ships or planes'. He notes that 'a high percentage' of the depth charges fired from ships were directed at whales rather than at submarines. 'The drifting carcasses of bombed or depth-charged whales were a common enough sight to lookouts aboard naval and merchant ships.'[17] The practice did not end with the war. Up to the late 1950s, the us Navy used whales for target practice during routine patrols for Soviet submarines.

Antarctic whales hardly had time to surface after the end of the war before the whalers returned. There had been a shortage of fats during the Second World War, and whaling nations were determined to profit from the southern oceans as soon as it was safe to sail.[18] Until the 1960s approximately 50,000 whales were removed from the Antarctic each year.[19] Radar, developed during the war, made the hunt more efficient. Once dead, the colours of the company and a radar screen were set up on the back of the dead whale. Carcasses could be found even in fog and darkness. With spotter planes, catcher boats and radar screens, a whale had a very small chance of surviving a chase.

In the spirit of international cooperation after the war, whaling nations gathered in Washington, DC, in 1946, one of the first formal attempts to control the resources of the open ocean. Before this, the seas beyond a nation's coastline had been considered *aqua nullius*, or belonging to no one. Only coastal whales, such as rights and greys, had been regulated. The newly established International Whaling Commission, or IWC, would attempt to control whaling well beyond a country's borders, in waters as remote as the Antarctic. To be effective, it would require unprecedented cooperation among nations.

The initial membership was composed almost entirely of whaling nations: Norway, South Africa, Great Britain, the United States, the Soviet Union, Japan, the Netherlands, Australia, Brazil, Canada, Denmark, France, Iceland and New Zealand. Other countries had an interest in whaling but were not actively hunting. The objective was to maintain a maximum sustainable yield of whales, by achieving the 'optimum level of whale stocks as rapidly as possible without causing economic and nutritional distress'. The overriding concern, in these years following the Second World War, was that humans should not suffer because of a decline in whaling.

Global quotas were defined in Blue Whale Units, or BWUS, which had been introduced by the Norwegians as a standard in

Liquid Whale fertilizer. By the mid-20th century, many whale products had been replaced by petrochemicals and spring steel, and the monster of the deep was little more than a global quota, expressed in Blue Whale Units.

1931.[20] Every whale killed was measured in terms of the average yield of oil for an adult blue whale, 110 barrels. Two fin whales were one BWU. Two-and-a-half humpbacks were one BWU. It took six sei whales to make a BWU. If the cultural history of the whale is shaped like an hourglass (or corset) – with a rich past of mythology and tradition and a current expansion of scientific interest in the whale – the 1920s to 1960s were the narrowest part of the waspiest waist. The monsters of the deep would be nothing more than a Blue Whale Unit. As Calasso wrote, with the coming of the Industrial Revolution, 'everything can be described as a moment in the cycle of production and consumption'.[21] Whales were no exception.

From the start, the BWU was a management failure. As blue whales declined, the fin-whale fishery expanded until the fins themselves were over-exploited. Sei whales were next. Since the quota was universal – that is, there was one communal limit set for all countries – a competitive system arose. Each whaling season began the race to catch as many whales as possible in the shortest amount of time. Haste encouraged waste, and whales were not fully processed. The number of catcher boats rose from 129 in 1946 to 263 in 1951.[22]

The narrow perception of the whale was not limited to industrialized societies. In the Arctic, the whale had been expected to suffer no more than the whalers did themselves through ritual and self-sacrifice. But such traditions were quickly lost with the introduction of firearms. The whalers brought southern commodities: rifles, ammunition, knives, sugar, tea, flour, tobacco and metal pots.[23] They also brought Old World diseases and the European approach to whaling. Soon after whalers arrived in the eastern Arctic, bowhead whales were hunted to near extinction.

For a winter's work, Inuit hunters might receive a small accordion or fiddle, food and a rifle. In some areas, Western instruments began to replace the caribou-skin drums used in healing rituals and festivals. The new music and firearms changed the approach to the hunt, whether it was for a bowhead or for smaller narwhals and belugas. A native of Baffin Island recalled:

> Singing was just an ordinary hunting method. The Inuit used to make up lots of songs – all kinds of different songs to make it easier to hunt the animals. They sang to get the animals used to the hunters. These people were very clever. We people now have guns; in the old days people just used their voices. No guitar, though![24]

The Arctic people themselves were changing. Traditional whaling dance songs were guarded secrets in some communities. But after commercial whalers arrived, Inuit travellers would sometimes be shocked to hear their village's songs performed hundreds of miles from home. In Alaska, some of these songs may have been learned in Jabbertown, a multilingual

Edward S. Curtis's photograph of Inuit drying whale meat at Hooper Bay, Alaska, *c.* 1929.

whaler's post near Point Hope.[25] In the eastern Arctic, old tribal boundaries were erased and territories shifted when substantial numbers of Inuit were transported by commercial whalers to hunt the whales and walruses of Hudson Bay.[26] The Canadian reporter Dorothy Eber wrote: 'The effects of the years that the whalers spent among the Inuit is perhaps still not fully realized . . . The relationship between Inuk and whaler was close and intimate; it is a rare Inuk who has no whaler ancestor.'[27] Traditionally, the shaman's power required a willingness to face danger – a shaman, or *angakoq*, might harpoon himself to exert his power over death. His power was obtained through 'dreams, visions and sickness'. In the early 1920s Ikinilik, an old Caribou Eskimo hunter, told Knud Rasmussen about the changes that had occurred among his people.

> Our angakoqs nowadays do not know very much, they only talk a lot and that is all they can do; they have no special time of study and initiation . . . I once asked a man if he was an angakoq and he answered: 'My sleep is dreamless, and I have never been ill in my life!'[28]

With the dreams went the invocations. Ikinilik continued:

> Now that we have firearms it is almost as if we no longer need shamans or taboos, for now it is not so difficult to procure food as in the old days . . . We forget what we no longer have use for. Even the ancient spirit songs that the shamans sing together with all the men and women of the village we forget, all the old invocations for bringing [Sedna] up to earth so that the beasts can be wrested from her – we remember no more.[29]

8 Exhaustion and Failure

Enticed by the riches that would come from vanquishing the whales, man disturbed the peace of their vast wilderness, violated their haven, wiped out all those unable to steal away to the inaccessible wasteland of icy polar seas . . . And so, the giant of giants fell prey to his weaponry. Since man shall never change, only when they cease to exist will these enormous species cease to be the victims of his self-interest. They flee before him, but it is no use; man's resourcefulness transports him to the ends of the earth. Death is their only refuge now.
Bernard Germaine Lacépède, French natural historian, 1804[1]

Marble would not be good enough to lay this corpse upon; for the sight – discard the blemishes – is wonder. This is the sordid remnant, yet the eye may even now replace what has been lost . . . Where went that spirit, which played in the magnificence – which made this mountain leap and sport, quickened the eye, retracted that balloon of a tongue, lifted that fallen jaw? This was a lump which solved some wild equation of the elements. This monstrous form and painted shapeliness has burned its way through phosphorescent waves in summer, the black night lighted by luminous clouds of its own breathing; and sinking with an easy silence, it has spiralled to unseen depths, upon unknown desires . . . It is more lovely and more startling than the Sphinx.
F. V. Morley, journalist, 1926[2]

By the end of the twentieth century, it appeared to many that Lacépède's prognostication on the demise of the whale was at last coming true. Foyn's harpoon gun, the stern slipway of the factory ship and the discovery in the Southern Ocean of the last great sanctuary of whales had helped to deplete every stock in every area of the globe. Only the diminutive minke whale seemed to exist in sufficient numbers to warrant an excursion.

Ommanney noted the familiar rhythm of whaling throughout the globe: it 'begins with a new discovery and hopeful enterprise, passing through a phase of fierce competition and ruthless exploitation with improving techniques and ended at length in diminishing resources, exhaustion and failure'.[3] The hunt on most whaling grounds was intense and short-lived. In their study of the bowhead whale fishery in the North Pacific, the whaling historians John Bockstoce and John Burns found that one third of all whales taken between 1848 and 1915 were killed in the first nine years of exploitation. Two-thirds were taken in the first two decades.[4] The whalers soon depleted the

Whaling in the Arctic greatly reduced right and bowhead populations by the end of of the 19th century.

Workers pose with a 20-metre bowhead whale in Kodiak, Alaska.

population, and the ships that continued to hunt in the late nineteenth century saw ever diminishing returns, their efforts eventually becoming futile.

The commercial hunting of bowheads caused famine on St Lawrence Island in the Bering Sea. The Danish ethnographer Kaj Birket-Smith, who travelled with Knud Rasmussen in the 1920s, noted the effect of the hunt in the Arctic:

> In earlier days whaling gave the Eskimos that reserve of meat and blubber without which the winter would prove hard. Up to twenty of these giants would be killed in a single season, and it was the rapid decrease in the numbers of right whales, when white whalers began their systematic butchery, which forced the government of the United States to introduce the reindeer into these regions, which had thus become almost bare of means of subsistence.[5]

Whales, and traditional whaling, disappeared throughout the North Pacific. The Koryak's hunt in the Sea of Okhotsk died out when whalers exterminated local bowhead stocks at the end of the nineteenth century.[6] In the Pacific Northwest, the Makah gave up whaling about the same time. Commercial whalers had hunted the once-abundant grey whale to near extinction in the breeding lagoons – about 3,000 kilometres south of the Makah hunting grounds.

How did this assault affect the creatures in the oceans? The Alaskan scientist A. M. Springer and colleagues have proposed that northern orcas became seal and otter eaters as a result of commercial hunting. Before they were ecologically exterminated, baleen whales were an important food source for gangs of these sleek, black-and-white carnivores, who took special interest in mysticete tongue. Once humans had removed the large whales, these adaptable predators moved to other, smaller meals.[7]

With the Arctic hunted out, industrial whalers moved on to the Southern Hemisphere. Approximately two million whales

After the decline of commercial whaling, many stations, such as these abandoned cookeries on South Georgia Island in the South Atlantic, are in ruins.

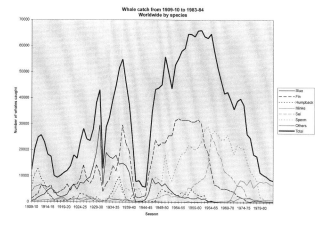

Whale catch from 1909-10 to 1983-84
Worldwide by species

Worldwide catches of whales by species, 1909–84. The decline in catches in the early 1940s was the result of World War II.

would be killed there in the decades that followed, 'a slaughter', according to the biologists Scott Baker and Phil Clapham, 'that has few parallels in the history of wildlife exploitation'.[8] In all, more than 350,000 blue whales were killed in the south;[9] by 1958 there were only about 4,000 left in all the southern oceans. As the blues disappeared, whalers looked for smaller prey: the fin whale, the smaller sei whales and the remaining humpbacks. Populations of humpbacks declined so rapidly that some were soon down to fewer than a hundred individuals.

Nonetheless, whalers continued to argue for the continuation of the practice. As late as 1958 the French whaling historian Paul Budker contended:

There are still a good many whales left – rorquals and sperm whales. Moreover, it is possible to claim that the larger cetaceans benefit from regulations – regulations that have been carefully considered and are planned to conserve the stocks while these are being exploited.[10]

143

This would become the refrain in the short sad ballad of industrial whaling – stocks can be conserved through exploitation.

Although the demand for sperm oil declined after the discovery of fossil fuels, technological advances in space exploration in the 1950s increased the demand for wax esters. With the US and the Soviet Union involved in a space race, the price rose fivefold, and the chase for the sperm whale became profitable again. By 1963 more than 20,000 sperm whales were killed each year to lubricate specialized machinery.[11]

Spermaceti, a stable wax ester, was used as a base for cosmetics in the 20th century.

Beauty's Diet. Pretty Billie Williams looks over cargo of spermaceti wax brought in aboard Anglo Norse. Once a useless byproduct of whaling, it is now prized as base for cosmetics. (NEWS foto by Peirella) —*Story on page 46*

144

The IWC could not curtail the slaughter: humpback populations were severely depleted and blue-whale populations were down to less than 1 per cent of historic levels. Until the mid-1960s fin whales formed the largest part of the worldwide catch, with about 20,000–30,000 individuals taken each year.[12] The take was far greater than the sustainable yield. Fin whales and then sei whales followed the familiar pattern of peak and decline. The last abundant great whales on earth soon became the target.

At 5 to 10 tonnes. minkes were so small compared to the traditional quarry of blues and fins that whalers had to re-outfit their ships. (Although they were not included in global oil quotas, it would take approximately 20 minkes to complete a BWU.) The 90-millimetre guns that whalers had developed for large rorquals would destroy a minke with a single shot. New harpoon guns were mounted on Japanese catcher boats, and 3,000 of the small cetaceans were caught in the first 85 days of operation. The whales were butchered largely for Japanese whale meat or pet food in Europe and North America, for bone meal, cosmetics and margarine.

The inability of the IWC to enforce its own regulations was perhaps most blatantly exposed by the Greek shipowner Aristotle Onassis. He fitted out a whaling fleet trained by Norwegians with a German crew, which operated under several flags, including Panama's. Although the Central American nation was an IWC member, it was incapable of exerting control over the shipping magnate. According to Ellis, Onassis's *Olympic Challenger* 'took endangered blue whales, female humpbacks and calves, and sperm whales so small that they had not developed teeth'.[13]

In a sense, Onassis's flagrant violations helped the conservationist cause. Here was a fantastically wealthy man bent on the destruction of whales for no apparent reason – he hardly need-ed the money. Onassis did not bow to international pressure, and he would not abide by treaties. For the IWC, and for whalers who claimed that their industry was strictly controlled and essential to the growing human population, he was a public-relations nightmare. Onassis seemed to relish the role of inter-national renegade: he invited American businessmen and socialites to watch whaling aboard the *Challenger*. The bar stools on his yacht were covered with the skin of sperm-whale penises, and whale teeth were used as footrests.[14]

In 1956 *Olympic Challenger* was dispatched to fish off the coast of South America, where Peru and Chile had just declared a 200-mile fishing limit. Onassis scoffed at the claim, which brushed up against accepted international law that was still based on a three-mile limit, once the maximum range of a can-non ball fired from the shore. The *Challenger* was seized by the Peruvian navy and retained until Onassis paid a $3 million fine. Since he had insured with Lloyds of London against such an eventuality, the incident caused him little economic pain. In fact, he made $12 million on the policy. But the global publicity – combined with a Norwegian court order to seize the ship and all its whale oil – persuaded him to sell the *Challenger* to Japan. The renamed *Kyokuyo Maru II* whaled in the Japanese fleet until 1970.

For most of the twentieth century, scientists were allied with whalers; much of their research was done either on the flensing deck or on the occasional stranded whale. Taxes levied on whale oil from the lucrative British Antarctic Territory financed exten-sive research in the Southern Ocean, including the natural history voyages of the RRS *Discovery*, the explorer Robert Falcon Scott's Antarctic vessel.[15]

Until the 1970s the expressed intent of this research was to gather biological knowledge to help the hunt. In some cases, the studies were intended to increase efficiency. Electric whaling – the transmission of a deadly shock through the harpoon – was first introduced in Bremen, Germany, in the 1850s. Research into this technique – an attempt to speed the immobilization of the whale, shorten the time of death and cause a rapid loss of consciousness – was rekindled in the 1930s.[16] In later years, the British Universities Federation for Animal Welfare lobbied for electric whaling, in the hopes that it would cause immediate unconsciousness in the whale, limiting its suffering. Yet there was one problem for whale-consuming nations: electrocution caused the meat to darken as a result of blood coagulation, spoiling its appeal.[17] In 1977 a Swiss drug firm suggested that fish anaesthetics and tranquillizers should be tested to anaesthetize hunted whales. But the plan was never realized, and the general acknowledgement that there was no way to dispatch a whale without pain became an accepted, if bitterly contested, reality.

From 1959 to 1969 special permits for hunting 316 grey whales – gone from the North Atlantic and almost extinct in the Pacific – were given to fishing companies in California. Although aerial surveys did census counts, the whales, which had been protected since 1946, were killed for data such as body measurements: length, width, thickness of blubber, size of baleen plates, number of ear-plug growth layers (an indication of age), condition of mammary glands, weight of testes and stomach contents. The research was to be used for a wise management programme, should commercial exploitation be resumed.[18] After the hunt, the whale meat was processed and sold, setting a precedent that has riled the IWC for decades.

In 1960 an independent committee of scientists was appointed to investigate whale stocks. The Committee of Three, Douglas Chapman of the US, K. Radway Allen of New Zealand

and the British biologist Sidney Holt representing the UN, analysed whale populations in the Southern Hemisphere, and their findings were tragic. There were fewer than 1,000 blue whales left in the world. Humpback populations were so low that scientists suggested that it would probably take 80 years of protection to restore their numbers. Yet the killing continued: in the whaling season of 1960–61, two Soviet factory ships removed almost 13,000 humpbacks from the waters south of Australia and New Zealand.[19] Two-hundred-and-fifty blues were killed during the whaling season of 1962–3.

The IWC meeting of 1963 in London proved a turning point. The global quota was lowered after an overwhelming number of scientific reports indicated that whale stocks had been hunted beyond sustainable numbers. Despite this, attempts to monitor pelagic whaling failed year after year. Two countries repeatedly ignored the regulations on Antarctic whales: the Japanese did not heed size restrictions, and Soviet whalers hunted outside whaling seasons, killing protected whales.

Although, at the time, the Soviets denied all charges of illegal whaling, following glasnost and the end of the Cold War, Russian scientists revealed that a titanic campaign of illegal whaling had been conducted since the 1940s. Secret whaling records showed that Soviet factory fleets killed every whale they encountered, ignoring size, age or protected status.[20] More than 700 right whales had been killed in the Sea of Okhotsk, even though the species had been protected since the 1930s. In the Southern Hemisphere, the difference between the reported take and actual catches was more than 100,000 whales.[21] At times, Soviet deception even included *over*-reporting their catch, to close down the whaling season early. With the ships of quota-abiding nations in port, Soviet whalers had the oceans to themselves to continue their harvest.

REPORTED VERSUS ACTUAL CATCHES BY THE USSR

	Reported	Actual
Blue	3,651	3,642
Pygmy blue	10	8,439
Fin	52,931	41,184
Sei	33,001	50,034
Humpback	2,710	48,477
Bryde's	19	3,212
Minke	17,079	14,002
Right	4	3,212
Sperm	74,834	89,493
Other	1,539	1,745
Total	185,778	261,646

After Soviet whaling came to an end, Russian biologists revealed that the USSR had been systematically engaged in illegal whaling (from Baker and Clapham's essay in *Encyclopædia of Global Environmental Change*, 2002).

Given the state of the whale industry and the evidence of illegal hunts, why couldn't international agreements be established to prevent the over-exploitation of the remaining whales? In their monumental *History of Modern Whaling,* J. N. Tønnessen and A. O. Johnsen summed up the problem in a single word – distrust. Whalers did not trust scientists and, without neutral observers, countries following the quotas did not trust others to comply. Rigorous self-enforcement of the quota system was seen as a way of giving other countries an advantage.

In the nineteenth century John Stuart Mill had argued that, in the marketplace, whales were fish, no matter what the zoologists said. In the age of industrial whaling, the gulf between biology and trade widened. Tønnessen and Johnsen wrote: 'it was impossible to bring biological interests in line with commercial interests'.[22] Commercial interests had the upper hand.

Many biologists viewed the whale hunt as irreconcilable with the reality of the oceans, but a growing number also saw it as an ethical failure. According to the cetologist David Gaskin,

> We could have conserved many other resources than just the stocks of large baleen whales, if the dead-end philosophy of the economic industrial growth ethic could be circumvented, and if the aces in the deck of cards with which we play were not invariably short-term economic gain and political expediency.[23]

Holt urged that the stress and pain of the chase, and even the grief caused to the companions of the hunted whale, should be taken into account in assessing the effects of the industry.[24]

And what of the fishermen – how did they take to an empty sea? Farley Mowat recorded the words of a Newfoundland fisherman, Arthur Pink:

> They was t'ousands of the big whales on the coast them times . . . So long as they was on the fishing grounds along of we, I never was afeared of anything; no, nor never felt lonely neither. But after times, when the whales was all done to death, I'd be on the Penguin grounds with nothing livin' to be seen and I'd get a feeling in me belly, like the world was empty. Yiss, me son, I missed them whales when they was gone.
>
> 'Tis strange. Some folks says as whales is only fish. No, bye! They's too smart for fish. *I* don't say as what they's not the smartest creatures in God's ocean.[25]

Perhaps they should have seen it coming. Had whaling nations patrolled themselves earlier, their hunt might never have become such a hot issue in the late twentieth century. After all, market forces – such as declining stocks and the rise of substitute products such as palm oil – were reducing the catch anyway.[26] But, threatened with the extinction of whaling, these nations ignored the shift in public opinion.

Still, they could not have seen the bright orange inflatables approaching on the horizon.

Once humans descended below the surface of the sea with cameras and hydrophones, their perception of whales changed.

9 Save the Whales

Before the 1960s, the most familiar image of a whale was probably that of a sperm bull putting up a fight – the ultimate foe, vanquished with courage and skill – or perhaps a raft of dead whales, lined up like the war dead beside a catcher boat. A few people might have seen a stranded whale on the beach or in an exhibition. But in the 1960s artists, photographers and scientists at long last revealed the way that whales spent 90 per cent of their lives.

Filmmakers such as Jacques Cousteau were revealing marine life as it had never been seen before. Using scuba technology that he had helped to develop, Cousteau made the marine environment familiar to millions of people. Charmed by his accent, television viewers watched frenzied sharks and stealthy barracudas from the safety of their living rooms. As early as his first book in 1953 Cousteau helped to dispel fear of the oceans. 'The monsters we have met', he wrote in *The Silent World*, 'seem a thoroughly harmless lot'.[1]

Using snorkelling gear and an underwater camera, the freelance photographer James Hudnall explored the Hawaiian breeding grounds of the humpback in the 1970s. His photographs provided a whale's-eye view of these 30-tonne rorquals, which he described as 'gentle, clever, passive, and rational beings'.[2]

His adjectives stuck. Never mind that male humpbacks can be quite aggressive towards each other in the breeding grounds. Humpbacks were gentle and endangered, worthy of concern. David Hill wrote in *Audubon* in 1974:

> The whale crisis has never been more acute. Each year the cost of killing whales goes up while the number of animals goes down. The economic squeeze has pushed most of the whaling nations out of the business. Two countries with sizable whaling fleets, Japan and the Soviet Union, stubbornly hang on. An industry historically plagued by greedy mismanagement of the resource does not have to give thought to the future of the industry because there is no future. But two critical questions remain: Will whaling cease of its own accord before or after species become extinct? Will the great majority of nations that no longer hunt whales sit idly by and allow the animals to go extinct?[3]

In the 1950s, while most cetologists were working on flensing decks, a few whale biologists, equipped with hydrophones – underwater microphones – began to record the complex sounds created by whales. The acoustician William Schevill made the first underwater recordings of cetaceans in the wild, describing the calls of more than 30 marine mammal species – from sperm whales to baleen whales, dolphins and seals. So extensive was his knowledge of these underwater sounds that Schevill helped to defuse a tense moment between the US and the Soviet Union during the Cold War. Consistent low-frequency blips had been detected in the oceans, and the Americans suspected that the Soviets might be using these sounds to locate US submarines. Schevill and his colleague William Watkins found the source: fin whales produce trains of blips for about fifteen minutes followed by a two- or three-minute pause, when they surface to breathe.[4] These sounds may have been used for echolocation, but fin whales were not considered a national threat.

The growth in understanding of great whales followed studies of their smaller relatives. The neurologist John Lilly described work he had done in the late 1950s with captive dolphins on the Caribbean island of St Thomas:

> the feeling was that we were up against the edge of a vast uncharted region in which we were about to embark with a good deal of mistrust concerning the appropriateness of our own equipment . . . The feeling of weirdness came on us as the sounds of this small whale seemed more and more to be forming words in our own language.[5]

Lilly went on to describe his subjects in his book of 1967, *The Mind of the Dolphin*:

> I wish to tell of what we have learned of a group of uninhibited nudists who have never worn clothes . . . They have no fireplaces, nor furnaces, or any fire at all . . . They have big brains and . . . they think enough of us to save each of us when they find us in trouble.[6]

The whale historian Paul Forestell explained the attraction of this new view of cetaceans to the youth of the 1960s: 'Sexually liberated, antimaterialistic, antiwar, self-sufficient, intelligent, and altruistic. . . . Lilly's message is clear – sun, surf, and sex – with big brains, and no guilt. Could it get any better?'[7]

Looking at the brains of baleen and sperm whales, you can see there is no doubt about capacity. The whale museum in Friday Harbor, Washington, has fin whale and human brains on

Behavioural studies of great whales followed research on their smaller relatives, such as captive dolphins. The consciousness of cetaceans played an important role in lobbying for their protection.

CELEBRATE
THE CONSCIOUSNESS OF CETACEANS
JOIN THE VICTORY FOR WHALES CAMPAIGN TO SEND ONE MILLION POSTCARDS TO WORLD LEADERS IN SUPPORT OF A PEACE TREATY FOR WHALES.
CETACEAN IS THE SCIENTIFIC NAME FOR THE FAMILY OF WHALES AND DOLPHINS.

display. The fin whale's brain looks like a plump turkey, whereas the human's might as well be an overcooked chicken. Cetacean brains are highly convoluted, like our own, but, unlike humans, whales have had a long time to get accustomed to their super-size grey matter. Cetaceans first evolved one-to-two-kilogram brains about 30 million years ago. We have had our 1.3 kilograms of neurons for a mere 100,000 years or so.

So what are they doing down there with all those brain cells? Certainly the complexity helps in hearing and echolocation (although it should be pointed out that bats have exceptional hearing and echolocation abilities, and their brains weigh little more than a gram). Lilly's thoughts on the importance of communication and intelligence in marine mammals influenced many budding cetologists. But as he turned from neurobiologist to mystic, many of these biologists were embarrassed to admit their debt to him. The legacy of Lilly's work survives in our love for the playful, intelligent whale, from dolphin to humpback.

Dolphins, those sleek cetaceans with the permanent smile, were the pioneering goodwill ambassadors for great whales. The film *Flipper* of 1963 had its roots in ancient Greek and Roman stories of a friendship between a boy and a wild dolphin. Before Flipper, whales in the cinema were mostly targets ripe for the harpoon, or dumb brutes, such as Monstro, mastered by fire. With few exceptions, cetaceans are heroes in post-*Flipper* films such as *Free Willy*, *Star Trek* IV: *The Voyage Home* and *The Core*. They help to save us.

In the dark world of the ocean, whales depend on sound for orientation. Lacking an external ear, they detect sound waves via a fat pad between mandible and middle ear. Often feeding beneath the euphotic zone, the surface of the ocean where light is dense enough for photosynthesis, whales use sound to find prey, locate mates and navigate the sea.

Sperm whales and most odontocetes echolocate – they emit sounds that enable them to detect distances and shapes. This ability is important for predators of the deep sea, where light is greatly reduced. Only 1 per cent of surface light travels to a depth of 100 metres; at 600 metres illumination equals that of starlight.[8] It is uncertain whether baleen whales, filter feeders, have this ability. The cetologist Peter Beamish has tested the ability of humpback whales to swim in the dark. He built a maze in a Newfoundland bay for a humpback rescued from a fishing net, then blindfolded the whale with rubber drain plungers. Before being set free, the humpback managed to navigate the maze.

Poets love the idea that whales see the world through their own vocalizations. The Australian poet Les Murray writes of the sperm whale:

> I sound my sight . . .
> With a sonic bolt from the fragrant
> chamber of my head, I burst the lives of some
> and slow, backwashing into my mouth. I lighten,
> breathe, and laze below again.[9]

To the American poet Amy Clampitt great whales

> . . . devise the ringing calculus
> of icebergs, compute the density of ships
> as pure experience of hearing . . . [10]

In the age of whaling, every hand on board would have been familiar with the sounds of blows. These deep exhalations, which could be frustrating in a fog when whales were obviously close but impossible to find. Some observers were puzzled by the flight response of distant whales to a harpooned one that they surely were unable to see. Occasionally, during periods of exceptional calm, whalemen might even hear the faint sounds of whales through the wooden hull of the ship.[11]

In 1967 the biologist Roger Payne began to record and analyse the sounds of humpbacks off Bermuda. Working from hundreds of hours of tape recordings taken on the breeding ground, Payne and Scott McVay contended that the sounds they heard were more than just idle chatter. They described the sounds as notes 'uttered in succession . . . to form a recognizable sequence or pattern in time'; in other words, they were songs with discrete themes.[12] All the whales in a breeding group

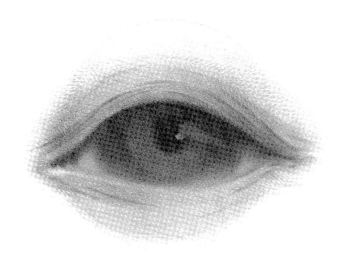

appeared to sing the same songs, over and over again.

The rhythms of humpbacks are similar to those of human music. Their songs last longer than our ballads but are shorter than most symphonies. Do they have an attention span like our own? Do they use similar techniques, repeating refrains that form rhymes, to remember songs? Payne and colleagues suggest that this is so. Our evolutionary path has been separated from whales for 60 million years. Perhaps we are latecomers to music, not the inventors of song.[13]

The humpback whale, coastal and slow-swimming, was familiar to whalers. To Scammon, the humpback had a 'roving disposition'.[14] Melville described it as 'the most gamesome and light-hearted of all the whales, making more gay foam and white water generally than any of them'.[15] It was this surface activity that made the humpback one of the first whales to catch the eye of whale watchers. Its scientific name, *Megaptera novaeangliae*, is derived from the Greek for 'big wing' – the humpback has exceptionally long flippers – and Latin for New England, the origin of the type specimen.[16] These mobile flippers make the humpback the most balletic of baleen whales. Naval engineers have shown that the scalloped leading edge of their appendages increases lift and decreases drag – a shape that could help in the design of aircraft and submarines.

In 1970 Capitol Records and National Geographic released *Songs of the Humpback Whale*. Payne's recordings became a smash hit, fascinating listeners around the globe; humpbacks soon became known as 'opera stars of the deep'.[17] Thirty years later, as I listened to the songs on a reissued CD, the hair stood up on my neck. With the eerie attraction of wolf calls, the recordings have lost none of their haunting novelty. At the same time,

The popularity of Roger Payne's recordings of the underwater calls of humpbacks helped change perceptions of whales.

the high-pitched squeals and moans evoked a vulnerability surprising in so large a creature. One Australian whaler declared that, had he heard those songs, he never would have 'fired a shot at a whale'.[18] The historian Barthelmess, on the other hand, recalled that he and the crew listened to Payne's recordings on the bridge of an Icelandic whaler while they were steaming out to the whaling grounds. 'It's a matter', he insisted, 'of culturization'.[19]

Humpbacks may be the pop stars of the ocean, but the loudest sounds produced by a living creature come from blue whales, which can communicate over a distance of 3,000 kilometres. Blue whales produce moans and gurgles four octaves below middle c, too low for human ears. Some scientists suggest that these calls enable them to echolocate, using the gullies and ridges on the ocean floor to navigate.

In the 1970s popular musicians such as Judy Collins and Paul Winter joined the chorus, recording with humpback accompaniment. The American composer George Crumb decided against mixing recordings with live music. In *Vox Balaena (Voice of the Whale)*, an electric flute, cello and piano create an evolutionary tale of the humpback. Beginning with a flutelike blow, Crumb used sounds based on seagull cries, whale songs and African chants to evoke the geologic past in five variations. The final movement, 'Sea-Nocturne (. . . for the end of time)', has an elegiac quality, dissolving into silence, or, as the musician Andrew Russo put it, 'the music dies down and evaporates into tomorrow'.[20]

In 1977 the songs of humpback whales were not only heard wheezing on turntables; the original songs of 1970 were compiled on a gold-coated phonograph record, along with greetings in 54 human languages, an elephant's trumpet and the roar of a rocket launch. It was attached to the side of the *Voyager 1* and *Voyager 2* spacecraft, in the event that they were intercepted by extra-terrestrial intelligence. They are now bound, according to Payne, on a billion-year journey to 'spread their message throughout the galaxy'.[21] En route, the probe would pass Sedna, a cold, ruddy planet discovered beyond Pluto in 2004 and named after the Arctic goddess.

For Payne, this galactic message accompanied a new awareness, an almost cosmological shift:

> When we have learned to accord the rest of life on earth equal rights, we can finally take our place in the court of intergalactic opinion and while holding our heads high claim: 'Yes, there is intelligent life on earth. And it is our species which demonstrates that the blind force of evolution is capable not just of self-destruction but of self-enlightenment.'[22]

In *Moby-Dick*, Judgement Day occurred aboard the *Pequod*. In Payne's book *Among Whales*, the judgement will occur in the court of inter-galactic opinion. The familiar religious forces are still at work. There is suffering (by the whales), epiphany (they're about to disappear) and redemption – we must save the whales from the harpoon and recognize that they have equal rights. This view challenges the whalers' perspective, in which whales and other animals do not have rights, a tradition that dates back at least to the Greek philosopher Porphyry, who noted that *nómos*, the law, does not extend beyond humans to the rest of nature.

In *Star Trek iv: The Voyage Home*, Judgement Day in the distant future does not go well at first. A black tube – described in one review as 'a colossal lipstick' – approaches Earth, ignoring all attempts by earthlings to make contact. After transmitting some unusual sounds, the tube creates a huge storm across the Earth's oceans, threatening all terrestrial life. Spock and Kirk decipher the tube's calls as those of the humpback whale, a species by then long extinct. So the crew travels back in time to 1986 to rescue two humpbacks who can answer the probe. Along the way, Kirk meets an attractive marine biologist and Spock swims with the whales (to ask their permission to take them forward in time). They assent not a moment too soon – foreign-speaking whalers, dressed in black, come barrelling down on the whales. The starship interferes in mid-harpoon.

In Disney's *Finding Nemo*, of 2003, the fish, the turtles, and even Jacques, the cleaner shrimp, speak English. But the whale – who swallows Marlin, the clownfish in search of his son Nemo – speaks only whale. Fortunately for Marlin, so does his sidekick, Dory. After her first attempt at communication fails, she tries a different dialect – humpback. The friendly leviathan gives the pair a lift to Sydney Harbour in his baleen-curtained mouth. We have come a long way from Monstro: the humpback poses small threat to the tiny passengers, permitting them to escape through his spout.

Since the 1960s books and films on whales have shifted away from the whaler's point of view, which had previously been ubiquitous. Christopher Ash's book of 1962 on whales and the fleets that pursued them was called *The Whaler's Eye.* Ash wrote of the whale: 'it is a beautiful creature when disporting itself at its leisure, and wonderful to see when running for its life'.[23] He was not joking. At the end of the decade, the biologist Victor Scheffer traced the imaginary journey of a sperm whale with her calf in *The Year of the Whale.* His book helped to weaken the already fading whaling lobby in the US.

With a sense of urgency I write about another kind of whale, before whales are remembered only from fading photographs and flickering videotapes. I write about sperm whales . . . Moving through a dim, dark, cool, watery world of its own, the whale is timeless and ancient; part of our common heritage and yet remote, awful, prowling the ocean floor a half-mile down, under the guidance of powers and senses we are only beginning to grasp.[24]

The whale-centred narrative was launched.

One of the first books to rouse the public was Farley Mowat's *A Whale for the Killing*, published in 1972, which emphasized the clash between traditional views and new sensitivities. Of the Norwegian whaling industry, still operating in Canada at the time, Mowat wrote: 'the stench of mega-death spread like a miasma . . . The Norwegian whaling industry had become a modern Moloch whose appetite was insatiable – and unrelenting.' His account of a fin whale trapped in a bay in Newfoundland condemned the cruelty imposed on the whale by locals determined to kill it for sport along with the entire iwc, 'a cynical device to divert the attention from the truth'. Mowat described the 'rending sense of loss' he felt after the captive whale was shot and tormented by locals: 'It was dark, and there was none to know that I was weeping . . . weeping not just for the whale that died, but because the fragile link between her race and mine was severed.'[25]

In 1975 a few activists, hardened by daring efforts to stop the testing of nuclear bombs in the Pacific, determined to disrupt the link between factory whalers and their prey. In small and manoeuvrable Zodiacs, the Canadian Paul Watson and colleagues took on the world's only whaling superpower – the Soviet Union – and its 230-metre floating factory, towering ten storeys above the tiny inflatables. In the first encounter, Watson

Greenpeace activists approach a Japanese whale ship in the Antarctic, c. 2001–2.

climbed atop a small sperm whale killed by the Soviets to be photographed, thus exposing to the world their non-compliance with international regulations. But Greenpeace was not interested in compliance: its goal was to stop all commercial whaling.

In subsequent battles, Greenpeace activists placed themselves between sperm whales and harpoons, attempting not only to bear witness but also to create a living shield. The Soviets, at times, fired directly over their heads. But more effective than the direct challenge was the use of mass media to convey their message. The Greenpeace president Robert Hunter wrote:

> With the single act of filming ourselves in front of the harpoons, we had entered the mass consciousness of modern America – something that none of the previous expeditions

had achieved. It was Walter Cronkite himself who intro-duced our footage to the mass TV audience, footage that was then run on every single television channel in the US and Canada, spilling over into Europe and even Japan.[26]

Greenpeace and other organizations later took on Australia (successful; whaling was suspended in 1978) and Japan (so far unsuccessful), helping to make the whale a symbol of environ-mental activism. The whale, as David Day wrote in *The Whale War* (1987), was

> at the heart of a guerilla war of resistance that has spread all over the world, it is the symbol of the ecology move-ment and emblematic of all species on the planet ... If this amazing animal, the largest ever to exist on the planet, cannot be saved from the ruthless exploitation of a hand-ful of men, what chance of survival have other species?[27]

The environmental movement rallied around certain flag-ship species, or charismatic megafauna, including lions, elephants and panda bears. Whales became the ambassadors of the oceans. Payne noted:

> As the largest animal, including the biggest dinosaur, that has ever lived on earth you could afford to be gentle, to view life without fear, to play in the dark, to sleep soundly anywhere, whenever and however long you liked, and to greet the world in peace – even to view with bemused curiosity something as weird as a human scuba diver as it bubbles away, encased in all that bizarre gear. It is this sense of tranquility – of life without urgency, power with-out aggression – that has won my heart to whales.[28]

As the biological and aesthetic value of whales rose, their consumptive value declined. In most Western nations, the idea of killing and eating whales became unacceptable. College students, faced with the monumental task of reading Melville's deathless prose beneath 'Save the Whales' banners, now found themselves rooting for 'the monster'. The death of the White Whale becomes a tragedy, Ahab a mote justly tangled in his own lines.

It was becoming clear to many people interested in saving the whale that the IWC would not willingly suspend the destruction of whale populations. At IWC meetings, proposals for a ten-year moratorium on all commercial whaling were tabled but failed to achieve the three-quarters majority necessary to pass the resolution. At the United Nations Conference on the Human Environment in Stockholm in 1972, environmental organizations recommended an international moratorium on whaling, asking the UN to intervene and 'declare whales the common heritage of mankind'.[29]

Protests were organized outside the IWC meeting the following year, with environmentalists calling for a ban on all products – including Russian vodka and Japanese cars and televisions – from whaling nations. At the meeting, a complete ban on hunting fin whales was on the table. The Japanese had already largely given up on this large, and now rare, species and had recently refitted a floating factory to hunt exclusively for small minkes. But the Japanese delegates were reluctant to allow any new bans on larger whales.[30] The American delegate argued that the

IWC cannot emerge from this Conference without committing itself firmly to end fin whaling if it is to maintain the credibility of the Organisation before the world . . . I do not believe that my Government will run the risk of affronting world opinion by continuing to take fin whales

. . . Are we here to serve the whaling industry or to serve the world?[31]

As these rhetorical questions were contested at the meetings, so were more concrete concerns: how many whales remained? How many had been killed? As the answers came in, outrage grew. The whaling zoologist C. H. Townsend estimated that approximately 37,000 sperm whales had been killed during 100 years of Yankee whaling.[32] Such estimates stood in sharp contrast to twentieth-century efforts: from 1950 to 1970 almost ten times as many sperm whales, 337,604 individuals, were killed in the North Pacific alone.

As environmentalists learnt the scale of the carnage, the composition of the IWC began to change. Non-whaling nations joined the commission in the 1970s, sometimes with the economic support of anti-whaling groups, and former whaling nations such as New Zealand, Australia and Britain became advocates for conservation. The US passed the Endangered Species Act, which placed a national ban on virtually all great-whale products. Biologists on the Scientific Committee, who were less dependent on the whaling industry, became more outspoken. Holt concluded that the Japanese whaling industry had no significant future, 'except perhaps in about fifty years time when the whale stocks might have recovered'.[33] When the Japanese objected strongly to the lower quotas suggested by the committee, they made it sound as if the industry were determined, as Jeremy Cherfas wrote in 1988, 'to wring the last pound of flesh from the whales'.[34]

In 1974 the rising frustration was expressed by a Mexican delegate who said: 'this Commission will be known to history as a small body of men who failed to act responsibly in the terms of a very large commitment to the world and who protected the interests of a few whalers and not the future of thousands of whales'.[35] Inherent in this statement was the value of the whales themselves, not to the hunters but to the survival of their own kind. This idea was still new; some moderate groups felt compelled to justify whale conservation as a prudent safeguard for the future of humanity. Among the many benefits of protecting whales, the British organization Friends of the Earth claimed that saving them would 'ensure an important supply of protein for future generations – when meat protein is certain to be scarce . . . it is our duty to preserve and foster the considerable food resources that whales could provide if properly managed'.[36]

That same year the BWU was suspended. Biologists on the IWC finally imposed the obvious: it was impossible to protect any species without restrictions specific to its stock. The whale could be saved only species by species, whale by whale.

For decades, the IWC had failed to adopt the suggestions of its scientists, using scientific uncertainties, according to Chapman and his colleagues, 'as a convenient means of maintaining advice for [setting] catch quotas too high and allowing hunting to continue for too long'.[37] That trend ended in 1979 when a proposal to end pelagic whaling for all species except minke whales was adopted.

Yet attempts to stop all commercial whaling faltered. Japan hired American lobbyists to counteract efforts to close down whaling. One former IWC commissioner from the US was paid more than $70,000 for his advice to the Japanese whaling lobby.[38] Japan was also accused of manipulating the votes of less-developed nations to fend off the moratorium. When Brazil decided to close down its whaling operations in 1979, Japanese trade pressure reportedly stopped the Brazilian government from implementing it. The South American nation abstained from the moratorium vote in 1981. In 1982 it voted against the commercial ban, permitting whaling to continue from its shores. Most of the meat was sold to Japan. The Brazilian newspaper *Folha de São Paolo* connected the decisions to a Japanese investment programme of $400 million in Brazilian agriculture.[39]

Given the way that *Moby-Dick* casts its shadow across the world of whaling, perhaps I can be forgiven for seeing a touch of Ahab in Japan's quest to continue commercial whaling. The millions of dollars offered to developing nations glitter like the Spanish gold piece nailed to the *Pequod*'s mainmast to entice the crew to raise the white whale. Japanese cash drew a few members to its side, but other nations refused to comply. The Seychelles minister of development, Maxine Ferrari, bristled at Japan's threat to withdraw funding for fisheries research, should the Seychelles side with anti-whaling nations. 'Such a situation does not represent co-operation but domination', she protested.[40] The Seychelles voted to stop commercial whaling.

In 1982 a ten-year moratorium on all commercial whaling was passed, scheduled to begin in 1986, to give whaling nations time to close their operations. The US enforced this ban by vowing to reduce the allocation of fishing rights in its waters to any country that reduced the effectiveness of the regulations. Korea, trawling about 300,000 tonnes of pollack per year from the Bering Sea but catching only 2,000 tonnes of whale, decided to comply with the moratorium.[41] Although Japan, Norway, Peru and the USSR originally lodged objections, today only Norway continues the commercial hunt for minkes – which is not to say that it is the only country that whales. Iceland and Japan continue the hunt under the guise of scientific research, exploiting a loophole in the original IWC by-laws.

Ironically, the US later used similar measures to protect the *right* to whale. When Japan attempted to disavow the aboriginal status of the Arctic Inuit hunt in 2002, the US retaliated by threatening to stop all petroleum shipped to Japan from Alaska. Japan backed down.

Arguments between commercial and biological interests in the nineteenth and twentieth centuries switched from questions of taxonomy to those of sustainability. In the twenty-first century, decisions on hunting whales may depend less on science than on motive: are whales conserved in order to be consumed or should they be preserved in their natural state? Or, do we just want to be entertained by them?

On a recent ferry ride across Cape Cod Bay, the captain announced that a humpback whale had been seen breaching off the bow of the boat. After the announcement, the passengers rushed to get a glimpse of the whale, and the ship broke course to get close to it. The young humpback launched itself out of the water head first, and then fell back with an enormous splash. Each time a further whale was spotted, everyone dashed to starboard or to port. You might have thought that we were an Arctic crew sallying through the ice to take a whale a century ago.

Many conservationists argue that whales are now worth more alive than dead: that is, the value of seeing a whale brings in more tourist dollars than a dead one ever could. Whale watching is a young industry. In 1955, after thousands of people were attracted to a lookout at Cabrillo National Monument in San Diego to watch migrating grey whales, the first commercial trip was launched, at $1 per person. Since the whaling moratorium of 1986, the number of excursions has rocketed. In 1998 nine million people went whale watching, spending more than a billion dollars on tours, tickets and souvenirs.[42] Eighty-seven countries now host whale-watching excursions, far more than conduct whaling. Anti-whaling activists point to a study indicating that more than 90 per cent of whale-watching tourists insist that they would not go whale watching in a country that conducted whaling.[43] Unconvinced that the two activities are exclusive, both Iceland and Tonga, which have whale-watching industries, are considering the resumption of a commercial hunt.

Despite the shift away from whaling, most people still regard cetaceans as a commodity. Forestell notes that 'while the general trait has been to an increasing effort to protect and conserve, the motivational basis for the change remains highly anthropocentric'.[44] Certainly many fishermen have discovered the practicality of bringing the 'oo-ers' out to the whales, cleaning up their boats for whale watching one day and gearing up for charter fishing the next.

It is Brendan, the patron saint of whales, and the friendly leviathan Jasconius who have emerged from the mists of history as the model for these human–whale relationships. Approaching whales and embracing them (if not saying mass on their backs) is a common goal of the new whale tourists. Occasionally, a young whale watcher will ask me, in my role as researcher, 'Can you pet the whales?' (As a general rule, unless obtaining a DNA sample, researchers don't get very close to their subjects, but I have to admit, when a curious calf once rubbed against our research boat in the Gulf of Maine, I did reach down to touch its taut black skin.) There is a public desire to reach out to living cetaceans. Yet the whale-watching industry, which has ridden the wake of the 'Save the Whales' movement, also has roots in a long tradition of cetacean circuses, exhibitions and travelling shows.

Just as the first encounters with whales were from shore – the whale was a blow on the horizon or a meal at the margin of the land – the first public exhibits of whales were of strandings. Barthelmess notes that whales have been exhibited for at least 2,000 years: a whale skeleton was shipped from Palestine to Rome for public display in the first century BC. Most of these

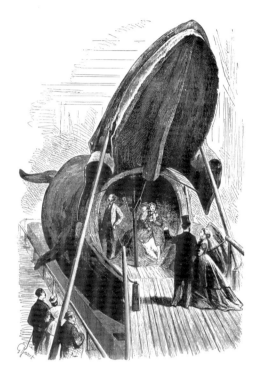

A blue whale stranded near Gothenburg, Sweden, was prepared with chemically treated blubber and exhibited in several European cities in the 1860s. Having tea inside the whale was a popular attraction for those who could afford it.

events were short-lived, since the smell was awful, although some entrepreneurs, unwilling to give up on their decaying stars, reduced them to bones and took them on the road. A team of oxen would cart the whale from town to town, where it would be reassembled, sometimes with great difficulty: the mandible of a baleen whale can weigh more than 250 kilograms.

One of the most celebrated was a 29-metre blue whale that stranded in the Netherlands in 1857. The Oostende whale, as it came to be known, was processed and articulated for a travelling exhibition. Although the showman, Herman Kessels, had made an agreement with the Dutch king to return the whale to his

A 29-metre blue whale stranded in the Netherlands in 1857 became the centrepiece of a travelling exhibition in Europe.

Whale exhibitions – of chemically preserved carcasses, not living whales – were often transported by rail in the late 19th century.

country when the exhibit ended, Belgium and the Netherlands split while the whale was on tour. Kessels, afraid that both kings would claim the whale, failed to return it to either of them. The bones are now to be found in St Petersburg.

At these exhibits, self-published newspapers and perfume were sold, the latter perhaps to quell the stench of rotting whale and to highlight the origin of ambergris.[45] The tradition of selling trinkets alongside whale exhibits has been retained by modern-day whale-watching excursions, where everything from key chains to T-shirts, videos and coffee mugs are available after a tour.

Such exhibitions combined entertainment with education. As far back as the seventeenth century, local crowds were urged to see the 'true and exact account and description of the monstrous whale'. A broadside of 1881 for the exhibition of a 'monster whale' in Philadelphia touted its educational value: 'no parent should neglect this opportunity to give the children so excellent and practical a lesson in natural history'.

Part education, part entertainment, targeting the human fascination with whales is a good way to earn a living: from 15 cents to see a skeleton in 1881 to £45 to see living minkes off Scotland or $2,000 to join a research project studying grey whales off the coast of California in 2004. Of course, the great difference between traditional exhibits and modern whale watching is that current commercial enterprises enable people to see cetaceans in their natural environment: a marine excursion might last an hour or two weeks; it might be from a kayak, fishing boat or helicopter; the tour operators might even encourage you to swim with the whales.

The distinction between an exhibit hall and the open sea is important. As the British literary scholar Jonathan Bate noted, 'We value nature for the very reason we are destroying it; the

Between 1880 and 1882 the Monster Whaling Association toured North America with a preserved blue-whale carcass taken off Newfoundland in 1880. The whale was one of several killed during an episode of experimental rorqual whaling out of Maine.

München   Oktoberfest   Theresienwiese!

RIESEN WALFISCH-AUSSTELLUNG

Kein Skelett! Vollständiger Walfisch, 22 Meter lang!
Grösstes Präparat der Welt.
Wissenschaftlich!   Belehrend!
Eintritt 20 Pfg.

A fin whale, harpooned off northern Norway, was chemically treated and exhibited as part of a German road show at the turn of the 20th century.

more we "tame" nature in our everyday lives, the more we value "wild" nature in our leisure time.'[46] Just as nineteenth-century broadsides touted the educational value of seeing a whale skeleton, whale cruises today often strive to strike a balance between education and entertainment. Joining a whale watch, tourists may be told that their voyage is part of a research programme, assessing the behaviour or population trends of resident cetaceans. They learn what whales eat, how they breed and

176

perhaps what whales risk from interaction with humans. In the end, whale watching extends from polite education to aggressive exploitation or even 'colonization', as Forestell calls it.[47]

Sitting on a beach in Cape Cod, I've spent hours watching right whales engaged in courtship activity: females with their dark flippers in the air and males chugging in from all over the bay. The whales were restless, the air filled with gruff blows – until the whale-watching boats got too close. Then the sea went quiet and the pod submerged. Although the whales later regrouped, the disturbance was evident at each close approach. Without strict guidelines, we intrude on their habitat.

Whales continue to intrude on what we consider to be our human habitat, washing ashore, dead or half-alive, in a terrible

A krill's-eye view: Richard Ellis's blue whale, constructed in 1968, hangs in the Hall of Ocean Life at the American Museum of Natural History in New York.

177

Whale watchers greet a grey whale off the coast of Baja, California. Just as 19th-century broadsides touted the educational value of seeing a whale skeleton, whale cruises today may strive to strike a balance between education and entertainment.

stink. A drift whale may once have been a royal fish, worthy of a small finder's fee going to the person who discovered the bounty. By the late twentieth century, a stranded whale prompted a call to the rescue squad. Farley Mowat recorded the response he got to his captive whale:

I was too tired to do more than glance at the mountain of letters from all over North America. Many of them contained small cheques and some held coins, gifts from all sorts of people: school children, the manager of a Chicago automotive works, a stockman from Calgary, a radio disc-jockey from New York, and a housewife from Labrador City . . . They begged me, sometimes in extravagant words, to save and free the whale. Some were sentimental; but the words were of no importance. What mattered was that these scattered and diverse people in far distant places had all been moved by one thing, by compassion for a strange, great creature, trapped and endlessly circling in a small pond on the remote coast of Newfoundland.

They gave me hope again.[48]

Strandings are still a great attraction, even if the response these days is with damp cotton sheets and front loaders for sending the creatures back to sea, rather than with flensing knives. A sperm whale came ashore on Fire Island, New York, in 1981. Nicknamed Physty, the whale was transported to a boat basin, where, according to Ellis,

he was fed (unsuccessfully), medicated (probably unsuccessfully), and televised (very successfully). He was released after a week's rest – probably the best thing to do for a stranded whale with pneumonia – and swam off into the Atlantic, never to be seen again.[49]

For the Maori of New Zealand, stranded whales once provided a vast amount of meat and oil, a gift from the god of the sea. Later, in the nineteenth century, desperate Maori joined the crews of European whale-ships. By the twenty-first century a stranded whale was a tragedy. In the New Zealand film *Whale Rider* of 2002, a Maori village weeps at the sight of stranded right whales, most of which are rather small, perhaps because animals closer to a human scale tug a bit more at the heartstrings. (Even an imagined whale requires distance to perceive it in the mind's eye.) The entire village tries to dislodge the stranded whales – a sign, as in medieval Europe, that all was not right with the world. Only a young girl succeeds, by riding into the surf on a right whale's back and re-enacting the

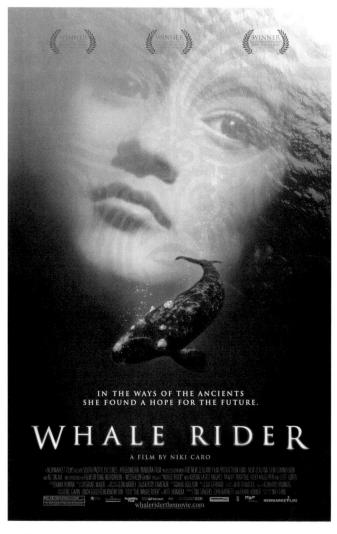

In Niki Caro's film *Whale Rider* of 2002, order is restored when a young Maori girl returns a stranded whale to the sea and saves her village.

journey of the mythical hero Paikia, who was carried to New Zealand on a whale. By returning the cetacean to the sea, the girl restores the morale of the Maori and their ancient relationship with the ocean.

When it is too late for a rescue, a dead whale rotting on the shore is considered a public health risk. What do you do with a 30-tonne animal when it washes up on a bathing beach? In its pamphlet 'Obliterating Animal Carcasses with Explosives', the us Forest Service recommends 3 lb of explosives for an 1,100-lb horse (cautioning the blaster to remove the horseshoes 'to minimize dangerous flying debris' and double the amount of explosives for 'total animal obliteration'). Someone should have warned the Oregon State Highway Division before it decided to obliterate a 14-metre grey whale from its shore. Half a ton of dynamite was placed on the leeward side of the whale, in hopes of dispersing the carcass in seagull- and fish-size pieces out to sea. The explosion showered the assembled

After being raised at SeaWorld, Gigi, a grey whale calf, was reintroduced to the Pacific in 1972.

crowd in blubber and whale guts, and one large slab smashed through the windshield of a nearby car.[50]

These days, few strandings have such explosive endings – although the occasional pick-up truck still sports a fading bumper sticker: 'Nuke the Whales' or, covering even more bases, 'Nuke the Unborn Baby Whales'. Instead, the carcass is towed out to sea or buried ashore, the bones retrieved for display in a local university or museum. Like the *hierozoika* of the Middle Ages, perhaps they help to sanction contemporary powers, in this case science and entertainment.

10 Eating the Whale

In the West, many countries stopped eating whale meat about the time of the rise of the whale-oil industry. The tongue was a Lenten meal, still considered a delicacy when the Basques hunted from their shores, but by the time that whaling went pelagic, the general public, and even whalers, rarely ate the meat. As Melville put it, 'when you come to sit down before a meat pie nearly one hundred feet long it takes away your appetite'.[1]

Some cultures have been eating whales for centuries. For present-day Norwegians, whaling may be a symbolic reminder of their glorious past, the days when they revolutionized and then dominated the industry. For the Japanese, eating whale may be a historical reminder of the role that whale meat played in saving the Japanese from starvation after the Second World War.[2] The German historian Klaus Barthelmess, claiming that human cultural diversity is just as endangered and worthy of protection as biodiversity, supports the resumption of whaling. Yet his is a rare voice in Germany, where his children have received death threats for his unorthodox views. At symposia on the history of whaling, however, he is not alone. In fact, the cultural divide between whaling historians and whale biologists seems as wide as the gap between whaling and non-whaling countries. Each faction tends to side with its research subject.

Hunter's Dilemma,
a stone-cut print
by Kavavaow
Mannomee, an
Inuit artist on
West Baffin Island.

For many cultures, the large balaenids were the preferred prey. Both northern right whales and bowheads could be hunted from shore and provided ample blubber and meat. In the twentieth century, after right whales had become endangered, and even the larger rorquals had become rare, some whale-eating nations switched to minke whales. The smallest of the rorquals, the minkes are at the centre of the whaling debate in the twenty-first century.

Legend has it that this whale got its name as the result of a Norwegian taunt. After a whale spotter named Meincke mistook the small rorqual for a blue whale, all the lesser rorquals became Minkie's whales. Finding no proof for this story, Barthelmess notes that the name actually comes from the Norwegian verb *minke*, which means 'to become smaller or reduce in size'.[3] It could just as well describe the recent trend in whaling.

Although the minke has been hunted since antiquity in Norway, where it was trapped in bays and darted with arrows infected with harmful bacteria, commercial whaling for minkes did not begin there until the 1920s. They became the primary source of whale meat in Japan only in the 1970s. Yet the size of the minkes has long made them popular prey for killer whales. In the Antarctic, they comprise up to 85 per cent of the diet of some orcas.[4]

In the 1980s Norway objected to the IWC moratorium and has hunted several hundred minkes per year despite the global ban. A founding member of the IWC, Iceland resisted the moratorium at first, but, under international pressure, the island nation suspended whaling in 1989. It recently resumed hunting minkes, justifying the annual take of 38 whales as an attempt to gather data on how much fish cetaceans consume. But of all whaling activities, Japan's pelagic hunt in the Southern Hemisphere remains the most controversial.

Iceland initially resisted the international moratorium on commercial whaling, but under international pressure it suspended hunting in 1989.

Japan has deep cultural ties with whales and whaling. Miyamoto Musashi was a noted 17th-century swords-man who fought 60 duels without defeat. Legend has it that he slew a whale single-handed. Woodblock print by Utagawa Kuniyoshi (1798–1861), *Miyamoto Musashi and the Big Whale*.

Japanese whaling dates back at least 1,000 years, originating in Neolithic prehistory. The development of harpoon whaling in the sixteenth century was followed by a uniquely Japanese method of hunting developed by Yoriharu Wada in 1677. Using large flax nets, hunters encircled a whale or mother-calf pair and lanced the entangled prey. Whalers then jumped astride the injured whale, carving holes and passing ropes through the blowholes and back. It is claimed that Wada got his idea from watching a spider web. This risky approach enabled hunters to attack species that were sometimes difficult to chase with harpoons. Net whaling continued in Japan for more than two centuries.

According to Ellis, Japanese whaling did not have the waste associated with the American and European hunt:

They ate the meat, used the oil for soap and lamps, but they also mixed the oil with vinegar to make an insecticide for rice paddies. The bones were crushed and used for fertilizer; the baleen for fans, fishing rods, lantern handles;

'Catching Whales at Gotō in Hizen Province', from *One Hundred Views of Famous Places in the Provinces*, 1859, colour woodblock print by 'Hiroshoge II' (Utagawa Shigenobu, 1826–1869).

A Japanese whale-oil factory at work.

medicines were made from various internal organs, and predictably, the penis was dried and pulverized into a tonic. The entrails were boiled into a soup, and it is said that the membranes of the heart were made into drum heads.[5]

Each whale was a highly valued prize, typically hunted for trade and not for local consumption. Guards were posted at whaling stations to prevent robbery, though many scrolls reveal that they occasionally ignored *kandara*, or petty theft, permitting elderly women and the indigent to steal a piece of whale. From a bounty that weighed several tonnes, a small piece of meat or blubber would not be missed.

Kujira was preserved by sun drying, salting and pickling. After the oil was removed, blubber was used to flavour soups. As in the North Atlantic, the most prized species was the right whale, *semi-kujira*. In some areas, onshore lookouts raised two smoke signals when they spotted a right whale, whereas most species warranted only a single flame. Sei and young fin whales

Japanese whales are often happy whales, even when advertising for restaurants serving *kujira*.

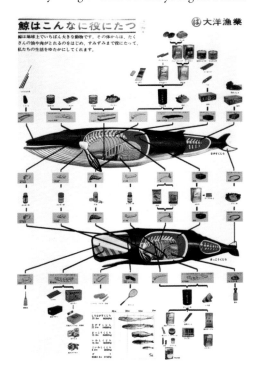

A Japanese poster illustrating the many products that come from baleen and toothed whales.

189

赤身の刺身

Sashimi (Akami)

also had high-quality meat, fetching good prices on the market.
Sperm whales were generally scorned, perhaps because of the
laxative properties of their meat.[6]

In parts of Japan, whales are lucky animals: eating *kujira* during the New Year's festival of Oshogatsu can bring good fortune
for the rest of the year. Whalers participated in many festivals

surrounding the hunt: dances were performed to prepare for the chase and to celebrate first the return of the whales and then the success of the hunt.

In the twentieth century, as coastal whale populations declined, the island nation embraced pelagic whaling. As the Basques may have done centuries earlier, the Japanese hired Norwegian whalers to teach them the trade, and Norwegian gunners worked on Japanese ships until the 1930s. Yet Japan was unique among factory whalers – it was the only nation to have food as the primary objective.[7] It is also the only industrial whaling nation to hold memorial services for whales killed in the hunt. For centuries, hunters had to repay the whales for giving their lives – and care for their souls. Some pelagic gunners still ask to be forgiven for taking a life. Unguarded souls could become *gaki*, hungry ghosts that caused illness or accidents at sea. In some communities, the souls of dead whales were treated with the same dignity as those of humans: they were given posthumous names, which were recorded on memorial tablets and included on death registers. Such stones have been found

With commercial whaling banned, Japanese whalers harvest minkes under the guise of scientific whaling.

from northern Hokkaido to the southern island of Kyushu. The sites of these memorials have become gathering places for the movement to protect whaling in Japan.[8]

Yet many outsiders feel that the sacrifice is misplaced. A *New York Times* editorial in 2000, for example, reprimanded the Japanese for the expansion of their whale hunt from the Southern Hemisphere into the North Pacific: 'Whale meat is not a staple in Japan, only a luxury food. The Japanese can make a small culinary sacrifice to preserve these majestic animals.'[9]

Japanese officials maintain that whaling and the consumption of whale is essential to their cultural identity. Yet pelagic whaling is far removed from the traditional shore-based stations that gave rise to the Japanese fleet. Most *kujira* comes from the Antarctic, and whaling is conducted by large companies, with scant connection to the traditional towns. At the same time, the officials insist that the hunt is for research only. According to Seiji Ohsumi, director general of the Institute of Cetacean Research, based in Tokyo, 'Non-lethal means for studying diets of whales simply do not provide the required data.'[10]

Critics of the whaling programme contend that whales are not killed for research but, rather, that Japanese research is conducted to kill whales. DNA analysis, for example, now allows scientists to track whale migrations across oceans, determine paternity and look into past population sizes – all with a skin sample smaller than a fingernail. In contrast, the Japanese research-whaling programme, which takes several hundred whales of 5- to 10-tonnes from the Antarctic and North Pacific each year, has published only a few papers on its work. Phil Clapham, a whale biologist in Woods Hole, Massachusetts, told the *New York Times* in 2002: 'This is a terrible record for a huge program that has been operating for years and killing thousands of animals for research.'[11]

DNA analysis has been used to probe the marketplace itself. In 1993 the whale biologist Scott Baker set up an impromptu genetics laboratory in a hotel room on the outskirts of Tokyo. Using a portable polymerase-chain-reaction, or PCR, machine, the workhorse of genetics research, he made synthetic copies of the DNA found in whale meat to bring back to the lab in Hawai'i. Although Japan had reported hunting only minkes, by 1999 Baker and his colleague Steve Palumbi compiled an inventory of species in the marketplace that would dwarf the life list of most whale watchers: nineteen fin whales, four Bryde's whales, two humpbacks, a sei whale, a blue whale, a blue-fin hybrid from Iceland, minkes and three species of beaked whales. Some of these species, such as humpbacks and blues, had been protected for decades. And new species are still showing up on the market: grey whale was recently discovered in Wakayama prefecture. A quarter of the samples sold as large-whale meat was actually from

Makah whalers flense a grey whale on the Olympic Peninsula, Washington, c. 1910–11.

dolphins and porpoises. These species are higher in the food web than baleen whales – and so their tissues have high levels of heavy metals and carcinogenic polychlorinated biphenyls, or PCBs. Although it was sold as clean, *kujira* now posed a health risk.

In 1995, on the other side of the Pacific, the United States announced that the Makah tribe of Washington State wished to take five grey whales per year for ceremonial and subsistence purposes.[12] The tribe had given up whaling in the 1920s, after grey whales had been hunted to near-extinction on their breeding grounds, more than a 1,000 kilometres south of the Makah reservation. But since the grey whale had recently been removed from the Endangered Species List, they wished to resume the hunt.

Anti-whaling activists were quick to respond. In a television interview, Paul Watson, the president of Sea Shepherd Conservation Society and a former member of Greenpeace, lambasted the proposal:

> The real reason for the initiative by the Makah is because they know very well that whale meat goes for $80 per kilo in Japan, and that one of those whales is worth close to a million dollars. So – what they have their mind set on here is a commercial whaling operation. And that doesn't mean just five whales that they say they want to kill . . . it will have implications for literally thousands of whales.[13]

There was, in fact, no evidence that the Makah planned to sell their meat abroad. But Watson was convinced that the hunt would erode the integrity of marine conservation in the US and reopen commercial whaling around the world.

An Iñupiak hunter waits for a bowhead in an umiak.

For many Americans, the Makah plan to use a .50-calibre rifle to kill the whale after it was harpooned was an affront to their traditional view of Native Americans as nature's stewards. The Makah quickly learnt the art of the press conference, appearing on the nationally broadcast *Today* show and on the front page of the *New York Times*. On 17 May 1999 they killed their first grey whale in three generations. Hundreds of aboriginal people came to eat the whale, but the celebration was brief. Not an ounce has been traded for profit. And not a single whale has been taken since.

From the first establishment of international whaling regulations, a distinction was made between commercial use and local consumption. At the Washington Convention of 1946, the hunting of right whales was prohibited worldwide, except for Alaska Natives, Canadian Inuit and Soviet Aleuts. Even these northern cultures, however, suffered from changes in the ocean ecosystem after decades of industrial whaling. When Thomas Peneahtak Brower visited the traditional whaling village of Barrow, Alaska, in 1928, he wrote: 'The village is like a deserted place today.'[14]

Jobs had been introduced to ward off famine, and these kept the men away from their homes. Whaling culture, at the centre of northern life for centuries, was on the verge of disappearing; many people predicted the doom of native customs.

But outsiders did not foresee the determination of these northern cultures to preserve their hunting traditions. Although aboriginal hunters had been given an exemption from IWC regulations in 1946, the moratorium on bowhead whales as adopted in 1978 suspended both commercial and traditional hunting in the Arctic. Protests by Alaskan Natives, and later by the US government, were successful, and a quota to strike eighteen whales was passed.[15] The notion of the cultural and nutritional survival of northern peoples in the form of whale hunting continues to have strong support from non-whaling nations.

The local disappointment with European food has been expressed since the whalers first arrived in the north, where bowhead *maqtaq* is the most treasured of all Arctic foods.[16] Although the Inuit traded blubber with whalers, the Europeans and Americans refused to give them money, preferring to trade food from the ship's stores, such as hardtack and salt pork, for whale: 'Usually on Saturdays', one carver recalled, 'the people

Among the Inuit whalers of Barrow, Alaska, the bowhead is butchered following strict customs that govern the distribution of shares.

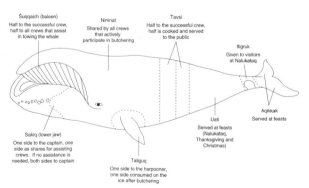

Suqqaich (baleen)
Half to the successful crew, half to all crews that assist in towing the whale

Nininat
Shared by all crews that actively participate in butchering

Tavsi
Half to the successful crew, half is cooked and served to the public

Itigruk
Given to visitors at Nalukataq

Aqikkak
Served at feasts

Uati
Served at feasts (Nalukataq, Thanksgiving and Christmas)

Sakiq (lower jaw)
One side to the captain, one side as shares for assisting crews. If no assistance is needed, both sides to captain

Taliguq
One side to the harpooner, one side consumed on the ice after butchering

would be given white man's food, but they would still be hungry for real food.'[17] An Iñupiak woman told the photographer Bill Hess about her time at a boarding school, when she was deprived of whale: 'The food was not filling. I got skinny, pale, sickly. We'll be sick around here this winter without whales.'[18]

The whale hunt is also a connection to the past. Each year in June, the Iñupiat celebrate Nalukataq, the formal whaling festival. Whales will give themselves only to hunters who share the catch with those who cannot hunt themselves. Successful crews distribute whale meat and *maqtaq* at the ceremony. Skins from the year's seal hunt are sewn together to form a blanket, and a hunter is tossed into the air when those holding it pull it taught. This blanket toss, which can lift hunters 10 metres into the air, is said to have its origins in the attempt to search for game across the tundra.

The Arctic hunt is defended by many biologists and whaling historians. Some social scientists take the argument further: whaling in this case is actually good for whales. The anthropologist M. G. Stevenson wrote:

> where human beings see themselves as an integral part of natural ecosystems, use is and can be an excellent conservation strategy. For example, both Inuit and scientists have recognized that whale populations that are hunted on a sustainable basis have less disease, more food, and reproduce faster than whale populations that are not hunted sustainably.[19]

Hard scientific data for such claims remain scant.

Although the bowhead quota has increased to 67 landed whales per year,[20] even just the *idea* of catch limits angers many Iñupiat in Alaska. As one whaling captain told Hess, 'A whale gives himself to a person that they feel deserves them. It's not the Iñupiat way to say you are going to get so many whales. You cannot put a number on it.'[21] Another complained: 'There's an old saying: You don't squabble over the bowhead whale. Whales sometimes send runners to check what's going on in the village.' In his frustration, however, the whaler revealed the secret that has helped to make this hunt one of the few examples of sustainable whaling in the twenty-first century: 'We have to be humble before this great animal.'[22]

11 Flukes

For whalers of old, a whale did not really exist until it had been struck, tried out, its capture stamped in the logbook, its individual worth expressed in the barrels of oil released from its blubber. For present-day whale biologists, whales do not exist until they've been photo-identified or, better yet, genotyped. Some research vessels resemble the early whaleboat. On the Bay of Fundy, the crew of the *Nereid* has one driver, two observers on the bow, ready to take photos when a whale is sighted, a data recorder, an alternate and a harpooner – or rather, an archer. Equipped with a crossbow or long bow, the modern boatsteerer is not looking for meat, of course, but for a skin sample.

Such a close association between researchers and the study animal sometimes brings the two together in odd ways. While tracking grey whales in Baja California in 1979, the cetologist Bruce Mate and a colleague got a little too close to a breeding pair, and the female got a little too close to them. As she was being pursued by a male, the cow took advantage of the small inflatable research boat, swimming upside down beneath the Zodiac. The male followed, his penis arched above the surface, and the researchers scrambled as the whale probed his penis into the boat. Mate said: 'We were used as a diaphragm by the female.'

Most relationships between whale and researcher are more distant and long-lasting. In their research into behaviour and social bonds, biologists rely on long-term studies of individual whales. Whales are identified using fluke and scar patterns, and in the case of right whales callosities, roughened skin that attracts cyamids and remains consistent through life. With the BWU finally abandoned, new whales are joining the list of historical and legendary cetaceans. To Moby Dick, New Zealand Tom, Shy Jack, Fighting Joe and Jasconius, we can now add a few names and personalities from the long list of whale research: Flyer, Mr Burns, Reflection, Stumpy (recently killed by a ship) and Sword. (One whaling historian has suggested that whoever names these whales should be flensed.)

An Iñupiat hunter reaches out to a grey whale trapped by ice off the coast of Alaska.

Through 'adopt a whale' programmes, conservationists have tried to broaden the fascination with whales into economic and political support for marine mammals. Trilobite B047 is a St Lawrence blue whale advertised for adoption on the Internet.

Eden, a Southern Hemisphere humpback, frequents the coast of Australia. She can be adopted for $35. Starry Night is an adult North Atlantic right whale who can be adopted through the New England Aquarium.

As Keiko, the star of the film *Free Willy* made clear, individual whales make good poster children. But most whales are simply identified by numbers or codes, which is not to say they are any less special. In 1935 a photograph of a right whale appeared in the *New York Herald Tribune.* After encountering a cow-calf pair off Brunswick, Georgia, a fishing crew had harpooned and shot the calf and then fired at the frantic mother. Six hours later, the calf was finally killed. The mother, injured but alive, swam off alone. Half a century later, the *Tribune* article came to the attention of Philip Hamilton and Scott Kraus at the New England Aquarium. With the help of a private investigator, they tracked

Photo identification of humpback flukes allows scientists to follow the lives of individual whales. Clockwise from upper left: Wide White Eyes, Twelve Ninety-Eight, Gertrude and Garfunkel. Gertrude is Twelve Ninety-Eight's mother.

down the original photograph and matched it to 1045, a 50-foot female seen off Cape Cod in the 1980s. Having lost her calf – the last right whale legally hunted in American waters – 1045 survived the bullet wounds and fifty years at sea, although she was never seen with a calf again.

After long days spent matching new photographs of callosities and flukes to a catalogue of existing whales, the researcher, like an old whaler, can find himself seeing whales everywhere. Melville:

> In bony, ribby regions of the earth, where at the base of high broken cliffs masses of rock lie strewn in fantastic groupings upon the plain, you will often discover images as of the petrified forms of the Leviathan partly merged in grass, which of a windy day breaks against them in a surf of green surges . . . Then again in mountainous countries . . . from some lucky point of view you will catch passing glimpses of the profiles of whales defined along the undulating ridges. But you must be a thorough whaleman, to see these sights.[1]

The researcher may also be privy to these visions. The peninsulas on the Maine coast take on the profiles of right whales rising from the ocean; a lift in the asphalt becomes a whale's back. Jasconius could be anywhere.

One of the most compelling new fields in whale biology has been the study of communication and culture. Toothed whales such as dolphins and sperm whales propagate sound waves to echolocate, but these sounds also indicate the presence of cultural lineages. Groups of killer whales maintain their own vocal dialects despite interaction with other groups. Dolphins appear to possess some of the core properties of grammar and syntax, fundamental to human language.[2]

The whale biologist Hal Whitehead has been observing sperm whales since 1987. Matrilineal groups, or clans, of these species appear to have distinct cultures and dialects. Some of these clans are restless or itinerant, travelling great distances in short periods of time. Others appear to be sedentary, remaining in one place for days. Whitehead transcribes the variation in vocalizations between clans: Group A 'Click-Click-Click-Click-Click', Group G 'Click-Click-Click-Click-pause-Click' and Group T 'Click-Click-pause-Click-Click'. Melville it is not, but these codas are preserved across the ocean and over time. Each repertoire, Whitehead noted, is 'a group property'.[3] Cultural inheritance in sperm whales is not only observed in their clicks and pauses but also in the variation in foraging patterns, synchronized dives, even defecation rates. To Whitehead, clan identity is similar to nationality in humans:

> like being a Slovenian, [clan membership] means not only being a member of a group with distinctive ways of communicating and behaving, but also knowing that one is a member of that group, which is different from other groups. Like humans in multicultural settings, sperm whales seem to show affinity for their own clan.[4]

Sperm whales may define themselves, if they define themselves, by what they are not. Membership in a dominant clan can increase the chances of survival and of reproduction.

Humpback whales also show evidence of cultural transmission. In any year, whales sing identical songs in Hawai'i and Mexico, breeding areas that are 4,500 kilometres apart. How do they manage this? Perhaps they hear the songs across long distances or learn them during the summer months, when different groups gather to feed. More remarkable than the geographic

consistency is the change in calls over time. Slight variations in the songs occur each year. But, as with evolution, these changes can make huge leaps in a short time. The Australian biologist Mike Noad and colleagues found evidence of a 'cultural revolution' in the Southern Hemisphere.[5] In 1996 two male humpbacks from the Indian Ocean arrived in the Pacific with a new song. Within two years, all the Pacific males had changed their tune, picking up the migrants' songs.

Why did they switch? A preference for novelty, perhaps, though this notion seems to be contradicted by the observation that all whales in a particular area sing the same song in a given year. Could there be a cultural aesthetic? Although the cause of this dramatic change is still unclear, our knowledge that cetacean cultures persist and change over time – and that culture is not the unique domain of humans – is likely to revolutionize our perception of these fellow mammals.

Yet whales, and our understanding of their calls, may be under a new threat. The oceans are getting noisier because of the constant hum and shriek of human traffic around the world. The US Navy now hopes to use high-decibel mid-frequency sonar to search for foreign submarines in the oceans of the world. These sound waves may not be as lethal as explosions, but marine mammals are at risk from such noise. Humpback whales change their songs in the presence of active sonar. And after a recent test of these signals, fourteen beaked whales stranded in the Canary Islands. Ten of them had gas bubbles in their blood vessels, evidence of decompression sickness, or the bends. The whales may have reacted to the ear-splitting noises by surfacing too quickly, disoriented by the sonar. Given that symptoms of the bends have never been found in these deep-diving whales, it is also possible that the noises caused the bubbles to form in the bloodstream of vulnerable whales.

A humpback male singing. Variation in whale songs is evidence that cetaceans have culture, which can change over time and vary across oceans.

In our quest to discover intelligence in whales, we often look for reflections of our own intellect. In the case of dolphins, this was done almost literally. When it became clear that dolphins could recognize themselves in a mirror, their self-awareness was widely celebrated.

But do we really love whales for how much they resemble *us*? And what about the traits we admire: their 'gentleness', sexual proclivity, musical ability and even capacity for a cultural revolution. When we praise whales are we poets, as the philosopher George Santayana might suggest, relishing our own verses?

Or have we begun at last to appreciate the cultural and biological diversity of the natural world? In Berlin in 2003 the iwc expanded its mandate, establishing a Conservation Committee to protect not just great whales but their smaller relatives, the dolphins and porpoises. Although controversial – 20 countries voted against the initiative – the iwc's focus has been extended beyond human economics and nutrition to include the conservation of cetaceans. All whales were included, and all countries welcome, whether they intend to whale or not.

Around the world, no-take zones, which restrict all fishing, are being created. Some biologists suggest that a global whale sanctuary would be appropriate, casting doubt that commercial whaling can ever be sustainable. Scott Baker observed: 'The past practice does not have much to recommend it.'[6] In whaling moratoriums, whale-watching restrictions and ocean sanctuaries, we can see a desire to restore the oceans to a mythical past before harpoons, before the impact of humans. For some, this past includes aboriginal hunts that rely on tradition, sacrifice and prayer. For others, sustainable consumption is a reasonable use of cetacean resources. Few, if any, argue for a return to industrial whaling.

And what of the whales themselves? The minke is once again abundant; the blue whale has returned to the Gulf of Alaska after a long absence. The right whale remains rare throughout the Northern Hemisphere, showing no signs of a rebound. Grey whales have been given full protection throughout most of their range. The whales seem to have warmed to these efforts. Once known as devilfish for their fierce determination to protect their calves, grey-whale mothers and calves now approach whale-boats, that is, whale-watching boats, for a session of light-sea petting by 'whale huggers' and tourists alike.

In an attempt to view the world from the whale's perspective, scientists attach tags to track their dives and migratory patterns. To evoke the voice of the whale, Crumb required that his performers wear visor-masks, dehumanizing their presence on the deep-blue stage. In *Reversing the Spell*, the American poet Eleanor Wilner imagines the whale's prayer for a future when the sea reclaims the earth:

Fluking right whale.

a great day when ships would all withdraw,
the harpoons fail of their aim, the land
dissolve into the waters, and they would swim
among the peaks of the mountains, like
eagles of the deep, while far below them, the old
nightmares of earth would settle
into silt among the broken cities, the empty
basket of the child would float
abandoned in the seaweed until the work of water
unraveled it in filaments of straw,
till even that straw rotted
in the planetary thaw the whales prayed for,
sending their jets of water skyward
in the clear conviction they'd spill back
to ocean with their will accomplished
in the miracle of the rain: *And the earth*
was without form and void, and darkness
was upon the face of the deep. And
the spirit moved upon the face of the waters.[7]

This is the spirit we seek when walking along an isolated shore:
the sight of a dark fluke above the surface or the faint, briny whiff
of whale drifting on the breeze. For a moment, just a moment,
the breath from the deep extinguishes any debate.

Timeline of the Whale

c. 47 million BC	*c.* 35 million BC	*c.* 40,000 BC	*c.* 2000 BC
Early whales, able to live on land and in water, begin their return to the sea	Toothed and baleen whales emerge in the late Eocene	Date of the earliest harpoons, developed to hunt the hippo-potamus in East Africa	Whaling developed among cultures in the Bering Sea

1620	1677	1819	*c.* 1825	1841
The *Mayflower* arrives in Massachusetts; whaling soon plays an important role in the New England economy	Japanese net whaling devel-oped by Yoriharu Wada	The whale-ship *Essex* is rammed and sunk by a sperm whale; the resulting tale – of deprivation and cannibalism – captures the contem-porary imagination of the dangers of whaling	Scrimshaw arises among Pacific Ocean whalers	Herman Melville voy-ages aboard the whaler *Acushnet*, bound for Cape Horn and the Pacif

1931	1946	1955	1970	1974
Blue Whale Unit, or BWU, is introduced by Norwegians as a measurement standard	International Convention for the Regulation of Whaling (ICRW) is signed in Washington, DC, lead-ing to the establishment of the International Whaling Commission (IWC) to regulate hunting and conserve whale stocks	The first com-mercial whale watch is launched in San Diego, California	Capital Records press-es 10 million copies of the album *Songs of the Humpback Whale*, recorded by Roger Payne; all hunted whales are listed as endangered in the US	BWU is sus-pended as a management tool

First century BC	AD 565–73	c. 1000	1596
Whale skeleton exhibited in Rome	St Brendan makes his legendary voyage to the Land of Promise, during which he is said to have celebrated Easter Mass on the back of Jasconius, a friendly whale	Basques begin the commercial hunt of right whales in the Bay of Biscay	Spitsbergen archipelago discovered by Willem Barents; reports of bowheads attract the Muscovy Company of England and hundreds of whale-ships to the northern waters

1851	1860s	c. 1909	1924	1930
Melville completes *Moby-Dick* in the Berkshire Hills of Massachusetts	The Norwegian Sven Foyn and the American Thomas Welcome Roys patent explosive harpoons; Foyn's harpoon cannon revolutionizes the whaling industry, exposing new species to exploitation	The conversion of whale oil to margarine begins on an industrial scale	The factory whaling ship, with stern slipway, is developed in Norway	The right whale is protected from commercial whaling

1975	1982	1986	1994	2003
Greenpeace confronts Soviet whalers in the North Pacific	IWC mandates a moratorium on all commercial whaling to devise an improved management system and to give depleted whale populations time to recover	Global moratorium on commercial whaling officially begins	Southern Ocean declared a whale sanctuary	IWC declares whale conservation as a primary goal

Appendix:
The Greenland Whale Fishery

This is the oldest extant whaling song in English, dating back at least to 1725. It was still being sung more than 100 years later, when it was transcribed aboard the whale-ship *Java*:

I can no longer stop on shore
Since I am so deep in debt
So a voyage to Greenland I must go
Some money for to get Brave Boys

Now Greenland it is a very cold coast
There is nothing but frost and snow
But it is the place likewise my boys
Where the whale fish blows Brave Boys

Our Chief Mate was at the main mast head
With a spy glass in his hand
Here's a whale, a whale, a whale fish he cries
And she blows at every span Brave Boys

Our Captain was on the quarter deck
And a very good man was he
Overhaul overhaul your davit tackle falls
And launch your boats to sea Brave Boys

Now the boats being lowered and all were man[n]ed
Resolved was each boat's crew
For to steer to sail to paddle and to row
To the place where the whale fish blows Brave Boys

Now the whale being struck and the line paid out
O he gave a splash with his tail
He capsized the boat and we lost five men
Nor did we get that whale Brave Boys

Now when the news to our Captain came
He called up all his crew
For the losing of these five brave men
He down his colors drew Brave Boys

Now the loosing of the five brave men
Did grieve his heart full sore
But the loosing of the fine Rite whale
It grieved him a d ** d sight more Brave Boys

From Stuart M. Frank, *Classic American Whaling Songs* (in preparation).

References

1 FIRST SURFACING

1 Kevin Crossley-Holland, trans., 'The Seafarer', in *The Oxford Book of the Sea*, ed. Jonathan Raban (Oxford, 1992).
2 Tim Severin, *In Search of Moby-Dick* (London, 1999), p. 12.
3 Ibid.
4 Ibid., p. 11.
5 Cornelia Catlin Coulter, 'The "Great Fish" in Ancient Story', *Transactions and Proceedings of the American Philological Association*, LVII (1926), pp. 32–50.
6 J.M.C. Toynbee, *Animals in Roman Life and Art* (Ithaca, NY, 1973), pp. 205–8.
7 Jorge Luis Borges, 'The Kabbalah', in *Seven Nights*, trans. Eliot Weinberger (New York, 1984), p. 102.
8 Klaus Barthelmess, 'Stranded Whales in the Culture and Economy of Medieval and Early Modern Europe', *Isana*, XXVII (2003), pp. 5–10.
9 Edmund Spenser, *The Faerie Queene* (1590).
10 Matthew XII, 39–41.
11 Paul Haupt, 'Jonah's Whale', *Johns Hopkins University Circulars* (1907), pp. 151–64.
12 Ibid.
13 Edmund Gardner, *His Journal and his Family*, ed. John Bullard (New Bedford, MA, 1958).
14 William M. Davis, *Nimrod of the Sea; or, The American Whaleman* (North Quincy, MA, 1972), pp. 351–5.
15 Haupt, 'Jonah's Whale'.
16 Methodius of Olympus, *On the Resurrection* (www.monachos.net/pascha/common/methodius_resurrection.shtml).

17   Stuart M. Frank, 'Whaling Literature', in *Encyclopedia of Maritime History* (in preparation).

18   Richard Ellis, *Monsters of the Sea* (New York, 1994), p. 192.

19   Geoffrey Ashe, *Land to the West: St Brendan's Voyage to America* (New York, 1962), p. 65.

20   Robert Van der Weyer, trans., 'Prayer of Saint Brendan', in *Celtic Fire: An Anthology of Celtic Christian Literature* (London, 1990), p. 30.

21   Coulter, 'The "Great Fish" in Ancient Story'.

22   John Milton, *Paradise Lost*, VII, 412–15.

23   Jorge Luis Borges, *The Book of Imaginary Beings*, trans. Norman Thomas di Giovanni (New York, 1978), p 96.

24   Richard Hamer, trans., 'The Whale', in *A Choice of Anglo-Saxon Verse* (London, 1970).

25   Rudyard Kipling, *Just So Stories for Little Children* (London, 1902).

26   Thomas Hobbes, *The Leviathan* (London, 1651), Introduction.

27   George Orwell, 'Inside the Whale', in his *Inside the Whale and Other Essays* (London, 1940).

28   Tom Waits, 'Starving in the Belly of a Whale', *Blood Money* (London, 2002).

29   Barthelmess, 'Stranded Whales', p. 6.

30   Stuart M. Frank, *Herman Melville's Picture Gallery* (Fairhaven, MA, 1986), p. 117.

31   Frank, 'Whaling Literature'.

32   Elizabeth Ingalls, *Whaling Prints in the Francis B. Lothrop Collection* (Salem, MA, 1987), p. 196.

33   Borges, *Book of Imaginary Beings*, p. 33.

2   THE INVENTION OF WHALING

 1   Randall R. Reeves and Tim D. Smith, 'A Taxonomy of World Whaling: Operations, Eras and Data Sources', Northeast Fisheries Science Center Reference Document 03–12 (2003).

 2   Klaus Barthelmess, 'Whaling and Sealing Worldwide', in *Whaling and Anti-Whaling Movement* (Tokyo, 1999), pp. 5–16.

 3   Ibid.

 4   John J. Burns, 'Arctic Marine Mammals', in *Encyclopedia of Marine*

Mammals, ed. W. F. Perrin, B. Würsig and J.G.M. Thewissen (San Diego, CA, 2002), pp. 36–45.

5 Asatchaq, *The Things That Were Said of Them: Shaman Stories and Oral Histories of the Tikigaq People*, ed. T. Lowenstein (Berkeley, CA, 1992), p. 9.

6 Franz Boas, *The Central Eskimo* (Washington, DC, 1888; reprinted 1964), p. 175.

7 Knud Rasmussen, *Across Arctic America* (New York, 1927), p. 195.

8 M.S.V. Douglas, J. P. Smol, J. M. Savelle and J. M. Blais, 'Prehistoric Inuit Whalers Affected Arctic Freshwater Ecosystems', *Proceedings of the National Academy of Science*, CI (2004), pp. 1613–17.

9 Hans-Georg Bandi, 'Siberian Eskimos as Whalers and Warriors', *Hunting the Largest Animals* (Edmonton, Alberta, 1995), p. 165.

10 J.C.H. King, *Artificial Curiosities from the Northwest Coast of North America* (London, 1981), p. 90.

11 *Final Report of the Inuit Bowhead Knowledge Study* (Nunavut, Canada, 2000), pp. 44–6.

12 George Vancouver, *A Voyage of Discovery to the North Pacific Ocean and Round the World, 1791–1795* (London, 1984).

13 Stefani Paine, *The World of the Arctic Whales: Belugas, Bowheads and Narwhals* (San Francisco, CA, 1995), p. 78.

14 James A. Ford, 'Eskimo Prehistory in the Vicinity of Point Barrow, Alaska', *Anthropological Papers of the American Museum of Natural History*, XLVII (1959), p. 151.

15 Edward William Nelson, *The Eskimo of Bering Strait* (Washington DC, 1983), pp. 257–8.

16 Joseph Lubischer, 'The Baidarka as a Living Vessel', *Occasional Papers of the Baidarka Historical Society*, I (1998).

17 Sam W. Stoker and Igor I. Krupnik, 'Subsistence Whaling', in *The Bowhead Whale*, ed. J. J. Burns, J. J. Montague and C. J. Cowles (Lawrence, KS, 1993), pp. 579–629.

18 See www.peabody.harvard.edu/Lewis_and_Clark/hat.html

19 Margaret Lantis, 'The Alaskan Whale Cult and its Affinities', *American Anthropologist*, XL (1938), pp. 438–64.

20 Ibid.

21 T. T. Waterman, *The Whaling Equipment of the Makah Indians* (Seattle, WA, 1920), p. 38.

22 Philip Drucker, *The Indians of the Northwest Coast* (New York, 1955), pp. 45–9.

23 Ibid.

24 Lantis, 'Alaskan Whale Cult', p. 452.

25 Edward S. Curtis, *The North American Indian*, vol. XI (Norwood, CT, 1916), p. 37. Line breaks by Debora Greger.

26 Ivan Veniaminov, *Notes on the Islands of the Unalaska District*, trans. B. Keen and Assya Kardinelowsky (St Petersburg, 1840), pp. 130–34.

27 Curtis, *North American Indian*, vol. XI, p. 23. Line breaks by Debora Greger.

28 Vinson Brown, *Peoples of the Sea Wind: The Native Americans of the Pacific Coast* (New York, 1977), p. 14.

29 Stoker and Krupnik, 'Subsistence Whaling'.

30 Lantis, 'Alaskan Whale Cult', p. 446.

31 Edward S. Curtis, *The North American Indian*, vol. XX (Cambridge, 1930), p. 141.

32 Margaret Lantis, *Alaskan Eskimo Ceremonialism* (New York, 1947), p. 50.

3 THE ROYAL FISH

1 Richard Ellis, *The Book of Whales* (New York, 1980), p. 44.

2 Herman Melville, *Moby-Dick* (New York, 1851), chapter 3.

3 Paul H. Forestell, 'Popular Culture and Literature', in *Encyclopædia of Marine Mammals*, ed. W. F. Perrin, B. Würsig and J.G.M. Thewissen (San Diego, CA, 2002), pp. 957–74.

4 Robert D. Kenney, 'North Atlantic, North Pacific and Southern Right Whales', in *Encyclopedia of Marine Mammals*, pp. 806–13.

5 Ibid.

6 Forestell, 'Popular Culture and Literature', p. 958.

7 Mark Kurlansky, *Salt* (New York, 2002), p. 111.

8 Richard Ellis, 'Whaling, Traditional', in *Encyclopedia of Marine Mammals*, pp. 1316–27.

9 Uwe Schnall, 'Medieval Scandinavian Laws as Sources for the History of Whaling', in *Whaling and History: Perspectives on the Evolution of the Industry*, ed. Bjørn L. Basberg, Jan Erik Ringstad and Einar Wexelsen (Sandefjord, 1993), pp. 11–15.

10 Ibid.

11 The Natural History Museum, London, http://www.nhm.ac.uk/zoology/stranding/history.html.

12 Heimir Thorleisson, trans. in *The Whale* (New York, 1968), p. 19

13 E. D. Mitchell, R. R. Reeves and A. Evely, *Bibliography of Whale Killing Techniques* (Cambridge, 1986), p. 56.

14 Richard Ellis, *Men and Whales* (New York, 1991), p. 51.

15 Ellis, *Book of Whales*, p. 45.

16 William Douglas, 1725, cited in J. A. Allen, 'The North Atlantic Right Whale and its Near Allies', *Bulletin of the American Museum of Natural History*, XXIV (1908), p. 285.

17 Jaap Bruijn, 'The Rise and Decline of Dutch Whaling in the 17th and 18th Centuries', *28th Annual Whaling History Symposium: New Bedford, MA, 2003* (unpublished).

18 Ibid.

19 Stuart M. Frank, 'Whaling Literature', in *Encyclopedia of Maritime History* (in preparation).

20 Cited in Charles M. Scammon, *The Marine Mammals of the Northwestern Coast of North America, Together with an Account of the American Whale Fishery* (1874) (New York, 1968), p. 195.

21 Ibid., p. 193.

22 Allen, 'North Atlantic Right Whale', p. 285.

23 Ellis, *Men and Whales*, p. 218.

24 John A. Cook and Samson S. Pederson, *Thar She Blows* (Boston, MA, 1937), p. 37.

25 Ellis, *Men and Whales*, p. 82.

26 Frank, 'Whaling Literature'.

27 Elizabeth Ingalls, *Whaling Prints in the Francis B. Lothrop Collection* (Salem, MA, 1987), p. 192.

28 Ibid., p. 9.

4 RAISING WHALES

1 Herman Melville, *Moby-Dick* (New York, 1851), chapter 24.

2 Edouard A. Stackpole, *The Sea Hunters: The New England Whalemen during Two Centuries, 1635–1835* (Philadelphia, PA, 1953), p. 122.

3 Steven Katona and Hal Whitehead, 'Are Cetacea Ecologically Important?', *Oceanography and Marine Biology Annual Review*, XXVI (1988), pp. 553–68.

4 Richard Mather, *Journal of Richard Mather* (Boston, MA, 1850).

5 Cotton Mather, *The Thankful Christian* (Boston, MA, 1717).

6 Ibid.

7 J. E. Rattray, *East Hampton History Including Genealogies of Early Families* (New York, 1953), p. 78.

8 Randall R. Reeves and Edward Mitchell, 'The Long Island, New York, Right Whale Fishery, 1650–1924', *Report of the International Whaling Commission*, X (1986), pp. 201–20.

9 Rattray, *East Hampton History*.

10 G. Jackson, *The British Whaling Trade* (London, 1978), p. 78.

11 Randall R. Reeves and Tim D. Smith, 'A Taxonomy of World Whaling: Operations, Eras and Data Sources', Northeast Fisheries Science Center Reference Document 03–12 (2003), pp. 23–8.

12 Stackpole, *Sea Hunters*, p. 20.

13 Ibid., p. 151.

14 Nathaniel Philbrick, *In the Heart of the Sea: The Tragedy of the Whaleship 'Essex'* (New York, 2000), p. 13.

15 Melville, *Moby-Dick*, chapter 14.

16 Cited in Charles M. Scammon, *The Marine Mammals of the Northwestern Coast of North America, Together with an Account of the American Whale Fishery* (1874) (New York, 1968), p. 203.

17 Cited in Stackpole, *Sea Hunters*, p. 30.

18 Elizabeth Hardwick, *Herman Melville* (New York, 2000), p. 2.

19 Enoch Carter Cloud, *Enoch's Voyage: Life on a Whaleship, 1851–1854* (Wakefield, RI, 1994), p. 27.

20 Philbrick, *In the Heart of the Sea*, p. 256.

21 Richard Ellis, 'Whaling, Early and Aboriginal', in *Encyclopædia of Marine Mammals*, ed. W. F. Perrin, B. Würsig and J.G.M. Thewissen (San Diego, CA, 2002), p. 1322.

22 Frank T. Bullen, *The Cruise of the Cachalot Round the World after Sperm Whales* (London, 1902), p. 9.

23 Ellis, 'Whaling, Early and Aboriginal', p. 1322.

24 Richard Ellis, *Men and Whales* (New York, 1991), pp. 171–2.

25 Dean C. Wright, 'The Commonplace Book of Dean C. Wright, Boatsteerer,

Ship Benjamin Rush of Warren, Rhode Island, 1841–45', in *Meditations from Steerage: Two Whaling Journal Fragments*, ed. Stuart M. Frank (Sharon, MA, 1991), p. 11.

26 Joanna C. Colcord, *Songs of American Sailormen* (New York, 1938).

27 Bullen, *Cruise of the Cachalot*, pp. 16, 20.

28 Nelson Cole Haley, *Whale Hunt: The Narrative of a Voyage* (New York, 1948), p. 14.

29 Elizabeth Ingalls, *Whaling Prints in the Francis B. Lothrop Collection* (Salem, MA, 1987), p. 140.

30 Owen Chase, 'Narrative of the Most Extraordinary and Distressing Shipwreck of the Whale-Ship *Essex* of Nantucket Which Was Attacked and Finally Destroyed by a Large Spermaceti-whale in the Pacific Ocean', in *Narratives of the Wreck of the Whale-Ship Essex* (reprinted New York, 1989).

31 George Pollard, 'Narrative of the Loss of the Whale-Ship *Essex*' in *Narratives of the Wreck of the Whale-Ship Essex*, p. 86.

32 Chase, 'Narrative of the Most Extraordinary and Distressing Shipwreck', pp. 50–51.

33 Ibid., p. 65.

34 Charles Olson, *Call Me Ishmael* (San Francisco, CA, 1947), p. 7.

35 J. N. Reynolds, *Mocha Dick; or, The White Whale of the Pacific* (New York, 1932).

36 Wright, 'Commonplace Book', p. 11.

37 Thomas Beale, *The Natural History of the Sperm Whale* (1835) (London, 1973), p. 166.

38 Bullen, *Cruise of the Cachalot*, p. 287.

39 Stuart M. Frank, 'Classic American Whaling Songs' (in preparation).

40 Cloud, *Enoch's Voyage*.

41 Mystic Seaport, recording aboard *Charles W. Morgan*.

42 Robert McNally, *So Remorseless a Havoc: Of Dolphins, Whales and Men* (Boston, MA, 1981), p. 94.

43 Bullen, *Cruise of the Cachalot*, p. 338.

44 Melville, *Moby-Dick*, chapter 67.

45 Ellis, 'Whaling, Early and Aboriginal', p. 1325.

46 Bullen, *Cruise of the Cachalot*, chapter 3.

47 Cloud, *Enoch's Voyage*, pp. 109–10.

48 Log of *Daniel Lincoln*, Kendall Whaling Collection, p. 301.

49 Joan Druett, *In the Wake of Madness*, (Chapel Hill, NC, 2003), p. 189.

50 N. Cushing, Kendall Whaling Collection, 1860.

51 Charles Weeks, Kendall Whaling Collection, 1830.

52 Druett, *In the Wake of Madness*, p. 228.

53 Aimee E. Newell, 'Fashions at Sea, Fashions at Home', *Piecework* (March–April 2003), pp. 54–7.

54 Alexander Starbuck, *History of the American Whale Fishery from its Very Inception to the Year 1876* (New York, 1964).

55 Emily Dickinson, *Selected Poetry of Emily Dickinson* (New York, 1997), p. xv.

56 Hardwick, *Herman Melville*, p. 8.

57 Harold Beaver, 'Introduction', *Moby-Dick*, Penguin Edition (New York, 1972), pp. 20–42.

58 Herman Melville, 'To Richard Henry Dana Jr,' in *Moby-Dick*, ed. Hershel Parker and Harrison Hayford (New York, 2002), pp. 532–3.

59 Tim Severin, *In Search of Moby-Dick* (London, 1999), p. 15.

60 William Gleim, 'A Theory of *Moby-Dick*', *New England Quarterly*, II (May 1929), pp. 402–19.

61 Ernest E. Leisy, 'Fatalism in *Moby-Dick*', in *Moby-Dick: Centennial Essays*, ed. Tyrus Hillway (Dallas, TX, 1953), p. 77.

62 Leonard A. Slade, Jr, *Symbolism in Herman Melville's* Moby-Dick: *From the Satanic to the Divine* (New York, 1998), pp. 1–25.

63 T. J. Jackson Lears, 'Reconstructing Nature: The Rise and Fall and Rise of the American Sublime, 1820–1920', in *Sargent: The Late Landscapes*, ed. H. T. Goldfarb, E. E. Hirshler and T.J.J. Lears (Boston, MA, 1999), pp. 3–33.

64 Severin, *In Search of Moby-Dick*, p. 15.

65 Melville, *Moby-Dick*, chapter 26.

66 Ibid., chapter 27.

67 Roberto Calasso, *The Ruin of Kasch* (Cambridge, MA, 1994), pp. 208–9.

68 Melville, *Moby-Dick*, chapter 24.

69 Joan Brewster, *'She Was a Sister Sailor': The Whaling Journals of Mary Brewster, 1845–1851* (Mystic Seaport, 1992), pp. 89–90.

70 Stuart M. Frank, '"Cheer'ly Man": Chanteying in *Omoo* and *Moby-Dick*', *New England Quarterly*, LVIII (March 1985), pp. 68–82.

71 Robert Cushman Murphy, *Logbook for Grace* (New York, 1947), p. 342.

72 Cloud, *Enoch's Voyage*, p. 95.

73 Frank, 'Classic American Whaling Songs'.

74 Dean C. Wright, Kendall Whaling Collection.

75 Melville, *Moby-Dick*, chapter 57.

76 Michael McManus, *A Treasury of American Scrimshaw: A Collection of the Useful and Decorative* (New York, 1997), p. 39.

77 Ralph Waldo Emerson, 'Boston', in *The Complete Works of Ralph Waldo Emerson* (Boston, MA, 1903–4), vol. XII, p. 186.

78 Melville, *Moby-Dick*, chapter 6.

79 Ibid.

80 Nathaniel Hawthorne, 'The Village Uncle', in *Twice-Told Tales* (New York, 1851).

81 George Francis Dow, *Whale Ships and Whaling: A Pictorial History of Whaling during Three Centuries with an Account of the Whale Fishery in Colonial New England* (Salem, MA, 1925), p. ix.

5 A DIVING MAMMAL

1 Aristotle, *Historia animalium*, trans. A. L. Peck (Cambridge, MA, 1965), p. 75.

2 John Stuart Mill, *System of Logic* (1843), cited in Harriet Ritvo, *The Platypus and the Mermaid and Other Figments of the Classifying Imagination* (Cambridge, MA, 1997), p. 49.

3 Herman Melville, *Moby-Dick* (New York, 1851), chapter 32.

4 Charles Francis Hall, *Arctic Researches and Life among the Esquimaux* (New York, 1865), p. 34.

5 Charles M. Scammon, *The Marine Mammals of the Northwestern Coast of North America, Together with an Account of the American Whale Fishery* (1874) (New York, 1968), p. 248.

6 Ibid., p. 251.

7 John Gatesy and Maureen A. O'Leary, 'Deciphering Whale Origins with Molecules and Fossils', *Trends in Ecology and Evolution*, XVI (2001), pp. 562–70.

8 Ibid.

9 D. R. Carrier, S. M. Deban and J. Otterstrom, 'The Face That Sank the *Essex*: Potential Function of the Spermaceti Organ in Aggression', *Journal of Experimental Biology*, CCV (2002), pp. 1755–63.

10 Melville, *Moby-Dick*, chapter 75.

11 Mark Cawardine, *Whales, Dolphins and Porpoises* (London, 1995), p. 55.

12 Sara J. Iverson, 'Blubber', in *Encyclopedia of Marine Mammals*, ed. W. F.
    Perrin, B. Würsig and J.G.M. Thewissen (San Diego, CA, 2002), pp. 107–12.

13 Ibid.

14 James L. Sumich, 'Blowing', in *Encyclopedia of Marine Mammals*, pp. 105–7.

15 Akito Kawamura, 'Plankton', in *Encyclopedia of Marine Mammals*,
    pp. 939–42.

16 Paul Dudley, 'An Essay upon the Natural History of Whales, with Particular
    Account of the Ambergris Found in the Sperma Ceti Whale', *Philosophical
    Transactions of the Royal Society of London*, XXXIII (1725), pp. 256–9.

17 Frank T. Bullen, *The Cruise of the Cachalot Round the World after Sperm
    Whales* (London, 1902), pp. 142–4.

18 Steven Martin, *The Whale's Journey* (Crow's Nest, Australia, 2001), p. 209.

19 E. A. Wilson cited in M. L. Oldfield, 'Threatened Mammals Affected by
    Human Exploitation of the Female-Offspring Bond', *Conservation Biology*,
    II (1988), pp. 260–74.

20 Katherine Ralls and Sarah L. Mesnick, 'Sexual Dimorphism', in *Encyclopedia
    of Marine Mammals*, pp. 1071–8.

21 Melville, *Moby-Dick*, chapter 88.

22 Hal Whitehead, *Sperm Whales: Social Evolution in the Ocean* (Chicago,
    2003).

23 Richard C. Connor, 'Ecology of Group Living and Social Behaviour', in
    Marine Mammal Biology: An Evolutionary Approach, ed. A. Rus Hoelzel
    (Oxford, 2002), p. 364.

24 Joan McIntyre, *Mind in the Waters: A Book to Celebrate the Consciousness of
    Whales and Dolphins* (New York, 1974), p. 122

25 Guillame Rondelet, cited and translated in Jacques Cousteau, *Whales*
    (New York, 1986), p. 193.

26 Sumich, 'Blowing', pp. 105–7.

6 OIL AND BONE

1 Vilhjalmur Stefansson, *Writing on Ice: The Ethnographic Notebooks of
   Vilhjalmur Stefansson* (Hanover, NH, 2001), p. 277.

2 Herman Melville, *Moby-Dick* (New York, 1851), chapters 42 and 119.

3 Ibid., chapter 68.

4 Sara J. Iverson, 'Blubber', in *Encyclopedia of Marine Mammals*, ed. W. F. Perrin, B. Würsig and J.G.M. Thewissen (San Diego, CA, 2002), pp. 107–12.

5 Richard M. Laws. 'Review of Encyclopedia of Marine Mammals', *Marine Mammal Science*, XIX (2003), pp. 599–606.

6 Hal Whitehead, 'Sperm Whale,' in *Encyclopedia of Marine Mammals*, pp. 1165–72.

7 Nelson Cole Haley, *Whale Hunt: The Narrative of a Voyage* (New York, 1948), p. 256.

8 A. J. Schulte, 'Altar Candles', in *The Catholic Encyclopædia*, vol. I (New York, 1907).

9 Richard Ellis, *Men and Whales* (New York, 1991), pp. 345–6.

10 Ambroise Paré, *On Monsters and Marvels*, trans. Janis L. Pallister (Chicago, 1982), p. 131.

11 Paul Dudley, 'An Essay upon the Natural History of Whales, with Particular Account of the Ambergris Found in the Sperma Ceti Whale', *Philosophical Transactions of the Royal Society of London*, XXXIII (1725), pp. 256–9.

12 Dale W. Rice, 'Baleen', in *Encyclopedia of Marine Mammals*, pp. 61–2.

13 Ellis, *Men and Whales*, p. 134.

14 Rice, 'Baleen'.

15 Harriet Beecher Stowe, *Uncle Tom's Cabin; or, Life Among the Lowly* (1852), chapter 36.

16 *American Heritage Dictionary*, 3rd edn (Boston, MA, 1996), p. 2030.

17 *Oxford English Dictionary*, New Edition (Oxford, 1998), p. 2298.

18 Andrew Dalby, *Dangerous Tastes: The Story of Spices* (Berkeley, CA, 2000), p. 67.

19 Ibid.

20 Dale W. Rice, 'Ambergris', in *Encyclopedia of Marine Mammals*.

21 Ibid.

22 Ibid.

23 Christopher Ash, *Whaler's Eye* (New York, 1962), p. 68.

7 FLOATING FACTORIES

1 Thomas W. Roys, Kendall Whaling Collection, 1860.

2 Alister Hardy, *Great Waters: A Voyage of Natural History to Study Whales, Plankton and the Waters of the Southern Ocean* (London, 1967), p. 31.

3 Robert Hendrickson, *The Ocean Almanac* (New York, 1978), p. 87.

4 C. Scott Baker and Phillip J. Clapham, 'Marine Mammal Exploitation: Whales and Whaling', in *Encyclopædia of Global Environmental Change*, ed. Ian Douglas (Chichester, 2002), pp. 446–50.

5 Cited in Phillip J. Clapham and C. Scott Baker, 'Modern Whaling', in *Encyclopedia of Marine Mammals*, ed. W. F. Perrin, B. Würsig and J. M. Thewissen (San Diego, CA, 2002), pp. 1328–32.

6 Ibid.

7 Paul H. Forestell, 'Popular Culture and Literature', in *Encyclopedia of Marine Mammals*, p. 959.

8 J. N. Tønnessen and A. O. Johnsen, *The History of Modern Whaling*, trans. R. I. Christophersen (Berkeley, CA, 1982), p. 268.

9 Ibid., p. 313.

10 Ibid., p. 228.

11 Farley Mowat, *Sea of Slaughter* (Shelburne, VT, 1984), p. 270.

12 Paul Haupt, 'Jonah's Whale', *Johns Hopkins University Circulars* (1907), p. 157.

13 Mowat, *Sea of Slaughter*, p. 258.

14 Farley Mowat, *A Whale for the Killing* (New York, 1972), p. 151.

15 Cited in Mowat, *Sea of Slaughter*, p. 250.

16 Mowat, *A Whale for the Killing*, pp. 54–9.

17 Gregory P. Donovan, 'International Whaling Commission', in *Encyclopedia of Marine Mammals*, pp. 637–41.

18 Forestell, 'Popular Culture and Literature', p. 959.

19 Richard Ellis, *Men and Whales* (New York, 1991), p. 365.

20 Donovan, 'International Whaling Commission', p. 638.

21 Roberto Calasso, *The Ruin of Kasch* (Cambridge, MA, 1994), p. 140.

22 Dorothy Harley Eber, *When the Whalers Were Up North: Inuit Memories from the Eastern Arctic* (Kingston, Ontario, 1989).

23 Nancy Wachowich, *Saqiyuq: Stories from the Lives of Three Inuit Women* (Montreal, 1999), p. 269.

24 Cited in Harold Seidelman and James Turner, *The Inuit Imagination* (New York, 1994), p. 145.

25 Thomas F. Johnston, *Eskimo Music by Region: A Comparative Circumpolar Study* (Ottawa, 1976), p. 75.

26 W. Gillies Ross, *Whaling and Eskimos: Hudson Bay, 1860–1915* (Ottawa, 1975)

27 Peter Pitseolak and Dorothy Eber, *People from Our Side* (Bloomington, IN, 1975), p. 38.

28 Cited in Seidelman and Turner, *Inuit Imagination*, p. 145.

29 Ibid.

8 EXHAUSTION AND FAILURE

1 Cited in Jacques Cousteau, *Whales* (New York, 1986), p. 13.

2 Cited in Richard Ellis, *Men and Whales* (New York, 1991), p. 223.

3 F. D. Ommanney, *Lost Leviathan* (London, 1971).

4 John R. Bockstoce and John J. Burns, 'Commercial Whaling in the North Pacific Sector', in *The Bowhead Whale*, ed J. J. Burns, J. J. Montague and C. J. Cowles (Lawrence, KS, 1993), pp. 563–77.

5 Kaj Birket-Smith, *The Eskimos* (London, 1959), p. 100.

6 Sam W. Stoker and Igor I. Krupnik, 'Subsistence Whaling', in *The Bowhead Whale*, p. 591.

7 A. M. Springer et al., 'Sequential Megafaunal Collapse in the North Pacific Ocean: An Ongoing Legacy of Industrial Whaling?', *Proceedings of the National Academy of Science*, C/21 (2003), pp. 12,223–8.

8 C. Scott Baker and Phillip J. Clapham, 'Marine Mammal Exploitation: Whales and Whaling', in *Encyclopædia of Global Environmental Change*, ed. Ian Douglas (Chichester, 2002), pp. 446–50.

9 Ibid.

10 Paul Budker, *Whales and Whaling* (London, 1958), p. 14.

11 Viktoria Schneider and David Pearce, 'What Saved the Whales? An Economic Analysis of 20th Century Whaling', *Biodiversity and Conservation*, XIII (2004), pp. 543–62.

12 Alex Aguilar, 'Fin Whale', in *Encyclopedia of Marine Mammals*, pp. 435–8.

13 Ellis, *Men and Whales*, p. 432.

14 Ibid., p. 433.

15 Alister Hardy, *Great Waters: A Voyage of Natural History to Study Whales, Plankton and the Waters of the Southern Ocean* (London, 1967), p. 36.

16 Edward Mitchell, 'Aspects of Pre-World War II German Electrical Whaling', *Report of the International Whaling Commission*, Special Issue 7 (1986), pp. 115–39.

17 Ibid.

18 Paul H. Forestell, 'Popular Culture and Literature', in *Encyclopedia of Marine Mammals*, p. 961.

19 Baker and Clapham, 'Modern Whaling', p. 1330.

20 Ibid.

21 Ibid., p. 1331.

22 J. N. Tønnessen and A. O. Johnsen, *The History of Modern Whaling*, trans. R. I. Christophersen (Berkeley, CA, 1982), pp. 632.

23 Forestell, 'Popular Culture and Literature', p. 961.

24 Cited in *Report of the International Whaling Commission*, Special Issue 7 (1986), p. 59.

25 Farley Mowat, *A Whale for the Killing* (New York, 1972), pp. 42–3.

26 Schneider and Pearce, 'What Saved the Whales?', pp. 543–62.

9 SAVE THE WHALES

 1 Jacques Cousteau, *The Silent World* (London, 1953).

 2 Paul H. Forestell, 'Popular Culture and Literature', in *Encyclopedia of Marine Mammals*, ed. W. F. Perrin, B. Würsig and J.G.M. Thewissen (San Diego, CA, 2002), p. 964.

 3 David Hill, 'Vanishing Giants', *Audubon Magazine*, LXXVII (1974), pp. 1–24.

 4 Roger Payne, *Among Whales* (New York, 1995), pp. 177–8.

 5 John Lilly, 'A Feeling of Weirdness', in *Mind in the Waters: A Book to Celebrate the Consciousness of Whales and Dolphins*, ed. Joan McIntyre (New York, 1974), pp. 71–7.

 6 John Lilly, *The Mind of the Dolphin: A Nonhuman Intelligence* (New York, 1967); reprinted in *Lilly on Dolphins* (New York, 1975), p. 291.

 7 Forestell, 'Popular Culture and Literature', p. 962.

 8 Sylvia A. Earle, *Sea Change: A Message of the Oceans* (New York, 1995), p. 112.

 9 Les Murray, 'Spermaceti', in *Translations from the Natural World* (New York, 1992), p. 44.

10 Amy Clampitt, 'Or Consider Prometheus', in *The Collected Poems of Amy Clampitt* (New York, 1997), pp. 89–90.

11 Roger S. Payne and Scott McVay, 'Songs of Humpback Whales', *Science*, 173 (1971), pp. 585–97.

12 Ibid.

13 Patricia M. Gray et al., 'The Music of Nature and the Nature of Music', *Science*, 291 (2001), pp. 52–4.

14 Charles M. Scammon, *The Marine Mammals of the Northwestern Coast of North America, Together with an Account of the American Whale Fishery* (1874) (New York, 1968), p. 45.

15 Herman Melville, *Moby-Dick* (New York, 1851), chapter 32.

16 Phillip J. Clapham, 'Humpback Whale', in *Encyclopedia of Marine Mammals*, pp. 589–92.

17 David Day, *The Whale War* (San Francisco, CA, 1987), p. 155.

18 Steven Martin, *The Whale's Journey* (Crow's Nest, Australia, 2001), p. 210.

19 Klaus Barthelmess, personal communication.

20 Andrew Russo, liner notes to George Crumb, *Voice of the Whale* (London, 2002).

21 Payne, *Among Whales*, p. 357.

22 Ibid.

23 Christopher Ashe, *Whaler's Eye*, (New York, 1962), p. vii.

24 Victor B. Scheffer, *The Year of the Whale* (New York, 1969), p. 5.

25 Farley Mowat, *A Whale for the Killing* (New York, 1972), p. 223.

26 Cited in Richard Ellis, *Men and Whales* (New York, 1991), p. 445.

27 Day, *Whale War*, p. 1.

28 Payne, *Among Whales*, p. 21.

29 Friends of the Earth, *Whale Manual '78* (London, 1978), p. 2.

30 J. N. Tønnessen and A. O. Johnsen, *The History of Modern Whaling*, trans. R. I. Christophersen (Berkeley, CA, 1982), p. 638.

31 Ibid., p. 676.

32 Ellis, *Men and Whales*, p. 32.

33 Jeremey Cherfas, *The Hunting of the Whale: A Tragedy That Must End* (London, 1988), p. 137.

34 Ibid., p. 137

35 Friends of the Earth, *Whale Manual '78*, p. 33.

36 Ibid., p. 5.

37 Cherfas, *Hunting of the Whale*, p. 146.

38 Day, *Whale War*, p. 108.

39 Ibid., pp. 106–7.

40 Ibid., p. 104.

41 Chang-Myen Byen, 'Whaling in Korea and Issues after the Moratorium',

Isana, XXVII (2003), pp. 11–16.

42 Erich Hoyt, 'Whale Watching', in *Encyclopedia of Marine Mammals*, pp. 1305–10.

43 E.C.M. Parsons and C. Rawles, 'The Resumption of Whaling by Iceland and the Potential Negative Impact in the Icelandic Whale-Watching Market', *Current Issues in Tourism*, VI (2003), pp. 444–8.

44 Forestell, 'Popular Culture and Literature', pp. 957–8.

45 Klaus Barthelmess, 'Cetacean Circuses and Mountebank Whales: The Commercial Exhibition of Whales from Classical Antiquity to the Present Day', *28th Annual Whaling History Symposium: New Bedford, MA, 2003* (unpublished).

46 Jonathan Bates, *Song of the Earth* (Cambridge, MA, 2002), p. 40.

47 Forestell, 'Popular Culture and Literature', p. 971.

48 Mowat, *A Whale for the Killing*, pp. 200–01.

49 Richard Ellis, *Monsters of the Sea* (New York, 1994), p. 200.

50 See www.perp.com/whale.

10 EATING THE WHALE

1 Herman Melville, *Moby-Dick* (New York, 1851), chapter 65.

2 Nancy Shoemaker, 'Whale Meat in American History', *Environmental History*, X (2005), pp. 269–94.

3 Klaus Barthelmess, personal communication.

4 Brent S. Stewart and Stephen Leatherwood, 'Minke Whale: *Balaenoptera acutorostrata*', in *Handbook of Marine Mammals*, ed. S. H. Ridgeway and R. Harrison (London, 1985), pp. 91–136.

5 Richard Ellis, 'Whaling, Early and Aboriginal', in *Encyclopedia of Marine Mammals*, ed. W. F. Perrin, B. Würsig and J.G.M. Thewissen (San Diego, CA, 2002), pp. 1310–16.

6 J. N. Tønnessen and A. O. Johnsen, *The History of Modern Whaling*, trans. R.I. Christophersen (Berkeley, CA 1982) p. 129.

7 Shoemaker, 'Whale Meat in American History'.

8 Arne Kalland and Brian Moeran, *Japanese Whaling: End of an Era?* (London, 1992), p. 155.

9 *New York Times*, 15 August 2000.

10 *New York Times*, 4 June 2002.

11 Ibid.

12 Randall R. Reeves, 'The Origins and Character of "Aboriginal Subsistence" Whaling: A Global Review', *Mammal Review*, XXXII (2002), pp. 71–106.

13 Robert Sullivan, *A Whale Hunt* (New York, 2000), p. 15.

14 Glenn W. Sheehan, *In the Belly of the Whale: Trade and War in Eskimo Society* (Anchorage, AK, 1997).

15 Bill Hess, *The Gift of the Whale: The Iñupiat Bowhead Hunt, a Sacred Tradition* (Seattle, WA, 1999), p. 8.

16 Stephen A. MacLean, Glenn W. Sheehan and Anne M. Jensen, 'Inuit and Marine Mammals', in *Encyclopedia of Marine Mammals*, pp. 641–52.

17 Penny Petrone, ed., *Northern Voices: Inuit Writing in English* (Toronto, 1988), p. 278.

18 Hess, *Gift of the Whale*, p. 8.

19 M. G. Stevenson, 'The Anthropology of Community-Based Whaling in Greenland', *Studies in Whaling*, IV (1997), pp. 3–15.

20 Us Federal Register (9 December 2002, LXVII/236).

21 Hess, *Gift of the Whale*, p. 15.

22 Ibid.

11 FLUKES

1 Herman Melville, *Moby-Dick* (New York, 1851), chapter 57.

2 Scott Norris, 'Creatures of Culture: Making the Case for Cultural Systems in Whales and Dolphins', *BioScience*, LII (2002), pp. 9–14.

3 Hal Whitehead, *Sperm Whales: Social Evolution in the Ocean* (Chicago, 2003), p. 286.

4 Ibid., p. 309.

5 Mike Noad et al., 'Cultural Revolution in Whale Songs', *Nature*, 408 (2002), p. 537.

6 Scott Baker, personal communication.

7 Eleanor Wilner, 'Reading the Bible Backwards', in *Reversing the Spell* (New York, 1998), pp. 156–7.

Bibliography

Bullen, Frank T., *The Cruise of the Cachalot Round the World after Sperm Whales*
(London, 1902)

Cawardine, Mark, *Whales, Dolphins and Porpoises* (London, 1995)

Ellis, Richard, *Men and Whales* (New York, 1991)

Hess, Bill, *The Gift of the Whale: The Iñupiat Bowhead Hunt, a Sacred Tradition*
(Seattle, WA, 1999)

McNally, Robert, *So Remorseless a Havoc: Of Dolphins, Whales and Men*
(Boston, MA, 1981)

Melville, Herman, *The Whale; or, Moby-Dick* (London, 1851) [now widely
available in critical editions]

Payne, Roger, *Songs of the Humpback Whale* (originally released in 1970; CD
available from www.livingmusic.com)

Perrin, William F., Bernd Würsig and J.G.M. Thewissen, eds, *Encyclopedia of
Marine Mammals* (San Diego, CA, 2002)

Scammon, Charles M., *The Marine Mammals of the Northwestern Coast of
North America, Together with an Account of the American Whale-Fishery*
(1874) (New York, 1968)

Scheffer, Victor B., *The Year of the Whale* (New York, 1969)

Tønnessen, J. N. and A. O. Johnsen, *The History of Modern Whaling*,
trans. R. I. Christophersen (Berkeley, CA, 1982)

Associations

AMERICAN CETACEAN SOCIETY
PO Box 1391, San Pedro,
CA 90733, USA
www.acsonline.org

GREENPEACE INTERNATIONAL
Ottho Heldingstraat 5, 1066 AZ
Amsterdam, The Netherlands
www.greenpeace.org

INTERNATIONAL FUND FOR ANIMAL-
WELFARE
PO Box 193, 411 Main Street
Yarmouth Port, MA 02675, USA
www.ifaw.org

INTERNATIONAL WHALING
COMMISSION
The Red House,
135 Station Road,
Impington,
Cambridge, CB4 9NP, UK
www.iwcoffice.org

NEW BEDFORD WHALING MUSEUM
18 Johnny Cake Hill,
New Bedford, MA 02740, USA
www.whalingmuseum.org

PACIFIC WHALE FOUNDATION
300 Maalaea Road, Suite 211,
Wailuku, HI, 96793, USA
www.pacificwhale.org

WHALE AND DOLPHIN CONSERVATION
SOCIETY
PO Box 232, Melksham,
Wiltshire SN12 7SB, UK
www.wdcs.org

WOODS HOLE OCEANOGRAPHIC
INSTITUTION
Woods Hole, MA 02543, USA
www.whoi.edu

Websites

Ambergris, a Pathfinder and Annotated Bibliography
   Complete guide to the renowned intestinal concretion of the sperm whale
   www.netstrider.com/documents/ambergris

Bioacoustics Research Program, Cornell University
   Whale vocalizations
   birds.cornell.edu/brp/SoundsMaMamm.html

Makah Tribe
   Includes links to traditional whaling and the grey whale hunt of 1999
   www.makah.com

Plough Boy Journals of Lewis Monto
   Includes numerous documents from nineteenth-century whaling. An extraordinary website, with Monto's journals, J. N. Reynold's 'Mocha Dick', Thomas Beale's 'Observations of Sperm Whales' of 1835 and much more.
   www.du.edu/~ttyler/ploughboy

WhaleNet
   Interactive educational website of whale research
   whale.wheelock.edu

Whale-Watching Web
   Provides hundreds of links, including sites for whale-watching companies
   www.physics.Helsinki.fi/whale

World Council of Whalers
   Includes whale recipes from whaling nations around the globe
   ww.worldcouncilofwhalers.com

Acknowledgements

Many valuable contributions were made by friends and colleagues interested in whales and the cultural history of whaling. Scott Baker, Klaus Barthelmess and D. Graham Burnett gave helpful reviews of chapters of the manuscript. I thank the series editor, Jonathan Burt, and the publisher, Michael Leaman, for bringing me on board. I would not have written this book without the assistance, encouragement and extensive research provided by Debora Greger.

The Whiteley Center provided a critical six-week residency at Friday Harbor, Washington. In Massachusetts, I had the great fortune of living near the New Bedford Whaling Museum and Kendall Institute during the writing of this book. Stuart Frank, director of the Kendall Institute, was extremely generous with his manuscripts and knowledge of whale history. I appreciate his copious responses to my many questions. Michael Dwyer, Laura Pereira, Michael Lapites, Suzanne Boudet and Hayato Sakurai were essential in helping me to complete the book. I salute the staff of the Ernst Mayr Library, Museum of Comparative Zoology at Harvard, for their help. Bob Woollacott and Marc Raila assisted with images. Randy Reeves, Bob Brownell and Phil Clapham provided historical and biological details.

That reluctant star, *Eubalaena glacialis*, the North Atlantic right whale and researchers at the New England Aquarium (especially Scott Kraus, Amy Knowlton, Philip Hamilton, Chris Slay, Lisa Conger and Marilyn Marx) helped to set me on this path more than a decade ago. It's been a wild ride. Laura Farrell provided editorial assistance, insight and, when I got swamped by images of floating factories, prompted me to go out and see some living whales.

Photo Acknowledgements

The author and publishers wish to express their thanks to the below sources of illustrative material and/or permission to reproduce it.

Photo American Museum of Natural History, New York: pp. 29, 177; collection of the author: pp. 14, 74; photo Hans-Georg Bandi: p. 33; photos Barthelmess Whaling Collection: pp. 12, 18, 23, 42, 48, 52, 62, 173, 175 (No. 939), 176, 186, 189, 190; photo Bjørn Basberg: 142; British Museum, London (photo British Museum): 50; photo Harry Brower, Jr: p. 196; photos Glacier Bay National Park & Preserve, Alaska: 201; photos Bill Hess: pp. 195, 200; John Klausmeyer: 105; Library of Congress, Washington, DC: pp. 22 (Prints and Photographs Division, LC-USZC4-10074), 39 (Edward S. Curtis Collection; lot 12328-b), 103 (Prints and Photographs Division, LC-USZ62-67681), 109 (Frank and Frances Carpenter collection, LOT 11453-1, no. 395), 128 (Prints and Photographs Division, lc-dig-ppmsc-06256), 129 (Coast Guard photo from the Office of War Information Photograph Collection; LC-USW33-029095-C), 130 (Coast Guard photo from the Office of War Information Photograph Collection; LC-USW33-029098-C), 137 (Edward S. Curtis Collection, lc- usz62-67382), 140 (Prints and Photographs Division, LC-USZ62-4618), 193 (Prints and Photographs Division, LC-USZ62-107820); Museum of Comparative Zoology, Harvard University, Cambridge, Mass. (collections of the Ernst Mayr Library): pp. 24, 37, 76, 100, 101; photos New Bedford Whaling Museum: pp. 11 (PZ-2756), 58, 59, 67, 79, 84 (logbook illustration ODHS-31), 89, 98, 118, 123 (foot), 125, 136, 144, 156, 185; photo New England Aquarium, Boston, Mass: 207; photo NOAA Library Collection: 110; photos The Peabody Essex Museum, Salem, Mass.: pp. 121, 174 (foot); photo Phillip Colla Photography: p. 6; photos Rex Features: pp. 131 (Jeremy Sutton Hibbert/Greenpeace/Rex Features, 379919BD), 165 (Rex Features, 379919

Index